What
SUCCESSFUL
MENTORS Do

There is no "one size fits all" professional development. Teaching is exciting and rewarding, but it is like pro football in that on any given day most anything may work, while on other days nothing seems to work. But you still need to keep on playing your best. Good mentors help keep good teachers playing at their very best. . . . As the authors so aptly suggest, good teaching is more a journey than a destination. This book will help both mentors and teachers to navigate this journey successfully.

Stephen Sroka, Health Education Consultants
Case Western Reserve University
Walt Disney Health Teacher of the Year
National Teachers' Hall of Fame inductee

What a great book to provide for all veteran teachers so that when we are chatting in the lunchroom and a "new" teacher shares a dilemma, anyone on staff can chime in with advice, backed by research and experience.

Diane Mierzwik, Teacher and Mentor
Parkview Middle School
Yucaipa, CA

Provides a wide range of practical suggestions for mentors that are based on current research and that can be "harvested" whenever needed. The "Precautions and Possible Pitfalls" sections serve as a welcome safety net, helping mentors to proactively examine and strategize solutions for anticipated challenges. The "Sources" sections are particularly helpful in offering additional readings for those mentors who are interested in going deeper into a topic. What Successful Mentors Do is easy to use, linked to best practices, and is certain to be an invaluable resource for new and returning mentors.

Theresa Ford, Developer/Consultant
Educational Testing Service, Downey, CA

What SUCCESSFUL MENTORS Do

81 Research-Based Strategies for New Teacher Induction, Training, and Support

Cathy D. Hicks ● Neal A. Glasgow ● Sarah J. McNary

CORWIN PRESS
A Sage Publications Company
Thousand Oaks, California

For information:

Corwin Press
A Sage Publications Company
2455 Teller Road
Thousand Oaks, California 91320
www.corwinpress.com

Sage Publications Ltd
1 Oliver's Yard
55 City Road
London EC1Y 1SP
United Kingdom

Sage Publications India Pvt. Ltd.
B-42, Panchsheel Enclave
Post Box 4109
New Delhi 110 017 India

Printed in the United States of America

Library of Congress Cataloging-in-Publication Data

Hicks, Cathy D.
What successful mentors do : 81 research-based strategies for new teacher induction, training, and support / by Cathy D. Hicks, Neal A. Glasgow, and Sarah J. McNary.
    p. cm.
Includes bibliographical references and index.
ISBN 0-7619-8886-6 (cloth) — ISBN 0-7619-8887-4 (pbk.)
    1. Mentoring in education. 2. Teachers—In-service training. 3. First year teachers.
I. Glasgow, Neal A. II. McNary, Sarah J., 1967- III. Title.
LB1731.4.H53 2005
370'.71'5—dc22

                                                              2004014432

This book is printed on acid-free paper.

05   06   07   08   09   10   9   8   7   6   5   4   3   2   1

Acquisitions Editor:	Faye Zucker
Editorial Assistants:	Stacy Wagner, Gem Rabanera
Production Editor:	Kristen Gibson
Copy Editor:	Ruth Saavedra
Typesetter:	C&M Digitals (P) Ltd.
Indexer:	Teri Greenberg
Cover Designer:	Michael Dubowe

Contents

Foreword

To say that I was pleased when the authors of *What Successful Mentors Do* asked me if I would be willing to write this foreword is an understatement. I was thrilled. In fact, I was honored. Every once in a while, something comes along in a field of research and practice that shows things more clearly and more accurately than before. This book is exactly that something in the field of education, more specifically, in teacher mentoring.

I have worked with many great educators during my 33 years in the profession. During my last 13 years in the San Dieguito Union High School District, I have been blessed with the opportunity to work with Cathy Hicks, Sarah McNary, and Neal Glasgow as their site principal. Taking their collective educational experiences in teaching, and in such mentoring programs as California's Beginning Teacher Support and Assessment program (BTSA), and putting them down in an easy-to-read, research-based format has created a gift for *all* educators. All three authors are hardworking, successful educators who live by the creed, "No one cares how much you know until they know how much you care."

The real gift of this book is that it can be read, understood, and implemented by educators at all levels. Whether you are a beginning teacher, a teacher who has been around awhile, or a site or district administrator, there are things to be learned and put into practice. As a school administrator, I have used topics from the book for staff development activities. The book's immediate benefit is obvious for teacher mentors, but teachers themselves can learn and change by working with the book's thought-provoking strategies.

There is one other reason I am excited about *What Successful Mentors Do* appearing in its entirety in print. It shows the depth of knowledge that Cathy Hicks, Neal Glasgow, and Sarah McNary have about teaching and learning behavior. For years, all of us who know these three individuals have thought of them as very good teachers, but far fewer people knew the depth and breadth of their knowledge and understanding of education. This book now opens up that extraordinary knowledge base to the entire profession. I know that teacher mentors will "lap up" this book. I also think it should be required reading in all teacher education courses.

I know that you will learn from this book. That is a given. But I hope you will also use what you learn. The advice and methods that Cathy, Neal, and Sarah give you in *What Successful Mentors Do* can change your paradigm in many areas of instruction and supervision. This book will make your school or your classroom a better place to learn.

Don Rizzi
Principal, San Dieguito High School Academy
Encinitas, California

Preface

Whenever people get really good at something, chances are that other people will see value in their expertise and try to model or emulate what they do. Think of apprentices with journeyman tradespeople, artists with mentors, physician interns with residents in teaching hospitals, postdoctoral fellows with senior scientific researchers; all are relationships designed to facilitate some exchange of information between the veteran professional and those promising newcomers just entering the field. Some of those relationships are informal. Others are arranged and precise, following a specific protocol for how the relationship is expected to work. Education is one of those fields that values and facilitates mentoring relationships. The expert-novice mentoring relationship has been around throughout human history.

In education, there are many examples of mentoring relationships. So why has so much attention been given to models of expert-novice relationships in education lately? First, the attrition rate among new teachers is high. And second, the job of teaching seems to be getting harder for a variety of reasons, and we in the institution of education have not done a very good job helping people make the transition from novice teacher to veteran teacher.

As mentors supervising new teachers, we want to be proactive rather than reactive. We want a vocabulary to describe and talk about what we both are experiencing. We don't want to miss common pitfalls or fail to "read" teaching/mentoring opportunities or challenging situations ahead of time. We don't want to miss large categories of induction topics we could or should cover. We want to achieve an "emotional literacy" to express empathy for those struggling with new educational scenarios. We want to be able to create and craft a highly effective educational environment to maximize the professional growth potential within the journey from novice to seasoned educator. Experience alone can be a slow teacher. With mentoring, we can do a better job than just providing new teachers with a place in which to work and gain experience.

So where do we as teacher mentors go to find out what works, what doesn't, and what works in one specific school setting (like yours) but not another? Unlike many other professions, the primary literature of educational research, experimentation, and investigation is usually a world away from the day-to-day grind of the classroom teacher. Rarely does that type of information filter into a teacher's professional life or development.

Yet that kind of information does exist. There is research on how teachers learn to teach, how new teachers are inducted into the profession, and how they are supervised, assessed, and evaluated. A simple keyword search of the literature can bring up a wealth of primary research sources and other information about new teacher induction, socialization, and induction relationships. Yes, there are others out there concerned about the quality of the induction experience for those new to mentoring and supervising beginning teachers. There is information supported by real data out there that can help define what works and what doesn't during this key period in a teacher's professional development. This information can make us all better at what we do.

Experience is a great teacher, but there are faster, more humane, and more efficient means of teaching and learning, which, when coupled with experience, become empowering, effective, rewarding, and beneficial. The purpose of this book is to give a voice to the research and the researchers who ask the important questions about new teachers, teacher support, and teacher induction and then find some of the answers. Filtered through our own experiences in schools, we hope to make the valuable products of research and inquiry available to all those involved in that crucial and important induction period. We have followed the trail of many investigations to address and cover as many of the important elements and principles of new teacher supervision and induction as possible. New teachers don't have to wait for experience to teach them; they can learn from the experiences of others, use what works, and avoid what doesn't. Then they can combine it all with what they already know and apply it in the classroom and school building.

This book is not meant to be read sequentially as one would read a novel. Rather, our objective is to focus on useful and practical educational research that translates into a range of choices and solutions to individual teaching and learning problems typically faced by new teachers and their mentors. Within our 10 chapters we present a large range of instructional strategies and suggestions based on educational, psychological, and sociological studies. The strategies are based on research done with preservice, student, or new teachers and with those supervising them. Strategies within the chapters are structured in a user-friendly format:

- **Strategy:** A simple, concise, or crisp statement of a mentoring or professional development strategy.
- **What the Research Says:** A brief discussion of the research that led to the strategy. This section should simply give the teacher mentor some confidence in, and a deeper understanding of, the principle(s) being discussed as a professional development strategy.

- **Application:** A description of how this strategy can be used in professional development and instructional settings.
- **Precautions and Possible Pitfalls:** Caveats intended to make possible reasonably flawless implementation of the strategy. We try to help teacher mentors avoid common difficulties before they occur.
- **Sources:** These are provided so that the reader may refer to the original research to discover in more detail the main points of the strategies, research, classroom, and professional development applications.

It is our hope that if those new to teacher mentoring and supervision accept some of these strategies, maybe they can avoid the "baptism by fire" or "sink or swim" mentality that many of us experienced when we first started working with new teachers. Veteran mentors can also benefit from knowledge gained from the most recent research. Given the critical need for new teachers now and in the future, as a profession we cannot afford to have potentially good teachers leave the classroom because they don't feel supported, they feel too overwhelmed, or they suffer from early burnout or disillusionment.

If you are a new mentor reading this book for the first time, there may be strategies that presumably don't apply. As in many new endeavors, a beginning mentor "may not know what you don't know." We ask that you come back and revisit this book from time to time throughout the year. What may not be applicable the first time you read the book may be of help at a later date. Veteran mentors can refresh their teaching and supervisory toolboxes by scanning the range of strategies presented in the book and selecting those applicable to their own mentoring environments.

Teaching, and education in general, have never been more exciting or more challenging than they are today. Expectations for teachers, students, and schools continue to rise. The more resources mentors have at their fingertips to assist new teachers along their educational journey, the better the outcome for all of us. We hope all mentors will find this book useful and practical in defining and enhancing their mentoring skills.

Acknowledgments

We are grateful to the people at Corwin Press, especially Faye Zucker, Stacy Wagner, and Cyndee Callan for their complete collaboration and support.

Cathy Hicks is grateful to Neal Glasgow and Sarah McNary for their experience and expertise in all aspects of their teaching. They are both professionals in every sense of the word. This has been a true collaborative effort, and they both made the experience most enjoyable. Cathy thanks all the mentors and teacher-leaders who have spent countless hours helping and advising their new colleagues in the learning process. Mentors are the lifeblood of teaching and provide valuable lifelines that bridge teacher preparation programs and the reality of 36 students in a class—all with different needs. Mentors never stop learning, investigating, reflecting, and growing in their own practice. They are the true heroes in teaching.

Cathy is especially thankful to her first mentors: parents Kim and Betty Daun, who taught her that hard work, determination, and a good education could take her far. Their love, patience, encouragement, and support are the greatest gifts she could ever receive.

And finally, an acknowledgment and thank you go to an incredible mentor, Mrs. Eleanor Bralver. A teacher at Sylmar High School in California, Eleanor is a dedicated teacher and role model for her students and other teachers. At age 90, she is the oldest full time teacher in the nation. Eleanor's passion for teaching and her desire to help students and novice teachers succeed make her an inspiration for all who know her.

Neal Glasgow gratefully acknowledges the now defunct The Science School, an alternative school-within-a-school where education came alive because of community professionals acting as mentors. It was a total "mentor" immersion and education in how it's done. Neal also acknowledges Dr. William Lennarz of the State University of New York at Stony Brook for clarifying the power of mentoring. Among his many accomplishments is a legacy of mentoring that turned countless science students and post-doctoral fellows into scientists. His down-to-earth style keeps it real.

Neal also acknowledges and thanks his co-authors, Sarah McNary and Cathy Hicks, for their insightful and professional contributions to this book, personal touch on mentoring, and their good humor. Because of them the messages in the book truly come from "the trenches of real mentoring." Their writing gives the academic research a "real world" validity and usefulness. Finally, he acknowledges Dr. Victor Chow of the University of California's Bodega Marine Laboratory and Reserve. While there are many mentor models out there, Victor Chow's teaching, learning, and mentoring style is still the standard by which Neal measures all others.

Sarah McNary is grateful to co-authors Cathy Hicks and Neal Glasgow for their confidence and expert suggestions, without which none of this writing would have been possible. Their dedication to education based on research rather than fashion is an inspiration to all the teachers they work with. Deepest appreciation is due to the students, student teachers, and beginning teachers she has worked with over the years. Working with all of them has been an honor and a delight.

Loving thanks go to Sarah's husband, Dave, and her children, Erica and Alex, for their support and understanding of the huge time commitment writing a book entails. Lastly, her deepest gratitude is extended to her sister, Jacqueline, who has made her believe that anything is possible.

Corwin Press thanks the following reviewers for their contributions to this work:

John Daresh, Professor of Educational Leadership, University of Texas, El Paso

Diane Mierzwik, Teacher and Mentor, Parkview Middle School, Yucaipa, CA

Hal Portner, Educational Consultant, Florence, MA

About
the Authors

Cathy D. Hicks is currently the Beginning Teacher Support and Assessment (BTSA)/Induction Coordinator for the San Dieguito Union High School District in Southern California. She oversees a two-year induction program for new teachers. She is the co-author of *What Successful Teachers Do: 91 Research-Based Classroom Strategies for New and Veteran Teachers* (Corwin Press, 2003). Cathy serves on the Executive Board of the California Association of School Health Educators (CASHE) and is on the adjunct faculty of California State University, San Marcos, teaching methods courses for teachers completing their credentials. She has presented at more than a dozen mentor-teacher leader conferences. Cathy has taught at both the middle and high school level for over 27 years. During that time she was involved in the California State Mentor Teacher Program and has been mentoring new teachers in her district for more than 19 years. Her energy, enthusiasm, and passion for teaching and supporting new teachers reinforce the career path she chose in elementary school. She believes the most effective teachers are the ones who never settle for "good enough" but continue to grow, stretch, reflect, create, collaborate, and take risks throughout their teaching careers. Cathy is married and has two grown children and one adorable granddaughter.

Neal A. Glasgow has been involved in education on many levels. His experience includes serving as a secondary school science and art teacher both in California and New York, as a university biotechnology teaching laboratory director and laboratory technician, as an educational consultant, and as a frequent educational speaker on many topics. He is the author of five books on educational topics: *What Successful Teachers Do: 91 Research-Based Strategies for New and Veteran Teachers* (2003), *Tips for the Science Teacher: Research-Based Strategies to Help Students Learn* (2001),

New Curriculum for New Times: A Guide to Student-Centered Problem-Based Learning (1997), *Doing Science: Innovative Curriculum Beyond the Textbook for the Life Science Classroom* (1997), and *Taking the Classroom Into the Community: A Guide Book* (1996). Neal is currently teaching AP art history and art at San Dieguito Academy High School, a California public high school of choice, and continues to do research and write on educational topics as well as work on various art projects. He is married, the father of two grown sons, and the grandfather of one grandson.

 **Sarah J. McNary** is currently teaching a credit recovery program for the San Dieguito Union High School District in Southern California, where she is also the district's consultant for special education working with the Beginning Teacher Support and Assessment (BTSA)/Induction program. She is a faculty member in the Masters of Education program for the University of Phoenix. Over the past 15 years she has taught SH, SDC, RSP, and general education classes at the elementary, middle school, and high school levels. She is a frequent presenter on a variety of aspects of special education and student support. She is innately curious and is a firm believer in lifelong learning. When asked what she teaches, Sarah will answer, "Kids"; when asked what she teaches kids, she responds, "Life! I just use my curriculum to do it!" She and her husband split their time between Encinitas and their mountain home. She is also the mother of two teenagers.

Introduction

*The Mentoring Process
Is a Journey, Not a Destination*

For those who are on the journey of mentor-teaching: There is a calling to share what we have learned (often painfully) to ease the way for those who are just beginning. There is a desire to teach, not just our students, but also those wonderful people who also seek to educate children. It is a noble calling and each of us has come to answer it in a different way.

Cathy Hicks

My own beginning teaching experience was as follows: "Here's the roll book, here's the keys, let me know if you have any trouble," and the door closed ominously. I don't think I saw the principal again until December.

I made it through that first semester. There were things that I should have done, and a few I shouldn't have. I was very idealistic about education and all that I had learned in college, but the reality—35 students, each with questions, concerns, and their own agendas—wasn't the perfect little class I had envisioned. There was so much more going on than just teaching the curriculum.

But there was one glimmer of hope. Jeannette Hill, a middle-aged PE teacher who taught the same period as I did, took me under her wing. She didn't provide me with lesson plans or even direction; she simply listened to my ideas and encouraged me to try them. In retrospect, I realize that she must have known what would work and what wouldn't; yet she never tried to dissuade me. Her positive attitude inspired me to keep trying until I got it right.

When I first became interested in mentoring, it was largely fueled by my desire to help people avoid some of the mistakes I had made. It's almost like raising children: You want your children to benefit from your experiences so they don't make the same mistakes you did.

In those days, mentoring was mostly stopping by, offering a kind word and an exchange of common sense ideas. Now we have programs that offer research-based support, concrete instructional models that have been tried and tested, and a commitment to professional development. A huge part of mentoring today is using a reflective practice in our formative assessment, which allows opportunities for growth over time. This encourages collaboration and communication among beginning and experienced teachers.

Neal Glasgow

My first real mentor was Vic Chow, an ecologist at Bodega Marine Lab. I thought I was there to learn science and science teaching. Instead I learned how to teach. I'm not talking about a two dimensional model; I'm talking about kids who learn like they are going to learn for the rest of their lives.

Vic believed in creating educational pathways that were guided tours for students to traverse. On those tours, the teacher served as a guide to help students realize their own learning—within their own style, at their own pace, and driven by their own motivation. The secret was to build curiosity and use it to inspire students to walk the path.

As a teaching assistant working with Vic, I was amazed by how enthusiastic his students were. And he made it look so damn easy! He's still one of the best teachers I ever knew. In my own career, I have always tried to stick to the basic framework of Vic Chow's style: carefully constructed educational environments developed with individuals in mind. When working with other teachers, officially mentoring or just supporting a co-worker, the goal is to be a coconspirator in constructing a viable educational environment. I am promoting the risk-taking that is essential to develop the self-discovery needed for teachers to find their own way and their own rewards while enabling the success of their students.

Sarah McNary

It was a Tuesday in late March 1997. I was walking back to my classroom after a 4:00 PM IEP meeting. The principal called out to me, "You're here late, can I talk to you for a minute?" I walked over to his office and he asked me to sit down. Then he asked me to consider applying for the position of site mentor. I was flattered that he thought I had what it took to help new teachers discover their strengths while navigating the muddy waters of lesson planning, classroom management, and the political nightmare of departmentalization. But I was nervous too. Could I really transfer my teaching experience into a product that was consumable by others? So much of my teaching "style" was guided by intuition.

I did apply that year and was elected by my peers, and all went well until I met my first group of six new teachers. They were a mixed group—science, special education, PE. All were knowledgeable about educational theory, but only two were prepared emotionally for the acid test of junior high.

I soon discovered that although I knew what they needed to do, I couldn't always put it into words for them. I also learned that my role was less "mentor" and more "chameleon." One day I was an expert on behavior modification, the next I was an amateur psychologist, then a cheerleader, followed quickly by my role as confessor. Their needs varied, not just from teacher to teacher or even class to class as I had expected, but day to day.

It's been seven years now since that first group made their maiden voyages into the world of education. Since then I've been a mentor teacher, an on-site university supervisor, and a mentor's consultant for the district. I've discovered that I am most effective not because of what I know but really whom I know. I'm not just talking about political connections—I'm referring to my ability to find information. Whether it's which secretary handles conference budgets, or which science teacher does the neatest labs, or what this year's research says about ADHD, I know how to find out. It's my connection to the needed information that makes me valuable.

This book was written to give you, as a mentor, the latest research on common issues faced by beginning teachers. It is an instant network of invaluable information. I know you'll find it most helpful.

1

Choosing the Best Strategies for Supporting New Teachers

"We cannot hold a torch to light another's path without brightening our own."

Ben Sweetland

 STRATEGY 1: Don't underestimate the rigors of the "induction" period for new teachers.

What the Research Says

 This study revealed that learning to become a mentor is a conscious process of induction into a different teaching context and does not "emerge" naturally from being a good teacher of children.

The study took place in Israel at a high school where the teacher-mentor worked as a teacher-leader within her English department. An English teacher in her 40s, with 15 years of teaching experience, was assigned a role as a mentor without any formal training. The research focused on one mentor and the process of learning to mentor to provide a more in-depth and substantial account of the subtleties and complexities of the process of learning to "read" mentoring situations.

"Reading a mentoring situation" in this context describes the forms and meanings that the mentor attributed to her first year of mentor induction. It is the case of how one experienced teacher in English learned to analyze one aspect of her learning in talking to mentor teachers of English about her formative stages of mentor induction experiences.

The metaphor for the mentored relationship is to compare the interactive process of reading, combining textual information with the information the reader brings to the text, as a dialog between the reader and the text. Thus we can interpret the mentor's evolving understanding of mentoring through the metaphor "learning to read the text interactively." The mentor as a "reader" is constantly interpreting and revising his or her own judgment of the meanings within the "mentoring text." This is done within the dynamic and unique nature of the dilemmas that the "mentees" face and manage. In the study's context, reading a mentoring situation could be interpreted as the evolving positioning of the mentor as she learned to reinterpret and reorganize her understandings of the dynamic nature of her practice. She learned to be more sensitive to the subtleties of the situation of her charge. This means knowing not just what any situation means but knowing what it means to the new teacher.

Application

What this research means to a beginning mentor is that learning to become a mentor is a conscious process of induction into a different teaching context and does not always emerge naturally from previous teaching experience with children. The study suggests that frustration, feelings of inadequacy, and uncertainties can be avoided by taking advantage of in-service opportunities or formal and informal "learning conversations" with fellow mentors mediated by more experienced mentors or mentors of mentors. The process of becoming a mentor reminds some of the development that new teachers' experience.

According to the research, the new mentor learns "to position him- or herself in relationship to his or her mentoring context by changing interpretive lenses as he or she encounters new situations." Further, "the various interpretive lenses the mentor wore, were characterized by transitions from initially being concerned with modeling her own teaching context in the new mentoring context, to concern for the way systemic factors (the technical and physical conditions of the workplace) affect the nature of the collaboration between mentor and mentees." These concerns transitioned to a concern with imposing the mentor's views on the mentoring agenda and, toward the end of the year, how systemic and interpersonal factors operate to affect the type and mode of collaboration that develops in mentoring interactions.

Teachers may remember a shift in their induction experience from a focus on their own performance to becoming more sensitive to individual pupils in their classrooms. A similar shift was noted in novice mentors becoming aware that "not everything is for everybody," which signaled a focus shift from their performance as mentors to a focus on attention to the particularities and diversity of the mentoring context and helping their new teachers discover their own teaching style.

Precautions and Possible Pitfalls

The study cited noted a developmental phase in which the new mentors began to express anger and "blame the system" for the strenuous beginning stages of their mentoring induction. Not every experience mentors have is going to be successful in their capacity as a mentor. They never seem to have enough time. Realize that this is just part of the total experience that most new mentors experience.

Source

Orland, L. (2001). Reading a mentoring situation: One aspect of learning to mentor. *Teaching and Teacher Education, 17,* 75–88.

 STRATEGY 2: *As a new mentor, be willing to exchange ideas with mentor colleagues as a means of professional development.*

What the Research Says

Professional development often consists of short workshops and inservices for teachers based on needs perceived by administrators and district office personnel. Professional development is something that is often done *for* or *to* teachers instead of *with* or *by* them. All too frequently this professional development may not enhance a teacher's classroom practice.

In a study exploring a group of teachers attending monthly meetings (McCotter, 2001), researchers found that it was possible to provide new and meaningful ways to build support and collegiality enabling continuous professional growth and development.

Members met monthly to provide support and feedback to one another. Support was expressed in several ways: having the opportunity to ask questions and pursue feedback, the sharing of similar experiences, suggesting solutions or strategies, or just showing support either verbally or nonverbally. The most important characteristics of these monthly meetings consisted of a "What is said in here, stays in here" pledge, group and individual reflection and critique, seeking feedback, and all-important collaboration. Group members felt this type of professional development helped them to reflect on their practice and experiences and more importantly had relevance and purpose for their classroom practice.

Application

Clearly a focus in education today is providing meaningful professional development for all stakeholders in schools. Because beginning mentors have needs and concerns that experienced veteran/mentor teachers may not have, it is important for them to feel supported and have their problems taken seriously. Many teacher-mentor induction programs are now providing professional development specifically designed for helping their beginning teachers. These programs are based on needs assessments given to new teachers and on surveying teachers with a few years' experience under their belts to determine what kind of professional development would have been helpful in the first year or so of teaching. Based on this feedback, districts are tailoring programs to meet specific needs.

Many new teachers feel totally intimidated around their experienced colleagues and might be cautious, if not downright reluctant, to discuss problems or concerns for fear of being perceived as weak or not in control. When new teachers can get together in a group and share problems and concerns with their peers, they realize they are not the only ones experiencing these questions or problems. The support can be as simple as giving practical suggestions for solving situations in the classroom or encouraging new teachers to step outside their comfort zone and try a new teaching strategy. The collegial communities that emerge from this ongoing support and collaboration can be lifesavers to a struggling mentor.

The use of reflective conversations with fellow teacher-mentors, as well as a mentor trained in the art of reflective conversation, can also be of great benefit. This reflection should be more than just thinking back on a problem or lesson; it should operate with the purpose of changing one's practice and enhancing students' learning. By engaging in these conversations in a nonthreatening environment, the beginning mentor has the opportunity to perceive himself or herself through a new teacher's eyes.

The importance of collaboration with colleagues cannot be overlooked. It is one of the most important components of good professional development for beginning teachers and mentors alike. If mentors new to the profession can share meaningful discussions involving a sharing of knowledge and focused on communities of practice, then as they progress from novice to experienced, confident veteran, the collaboration may well continue throughout their professional careers. The benefits, both personal and professional, to new mentors cannot be ignored.

Precautions and Possible Pitfalls

 New mentors should be aware that professional development is not a one-size-fits-all proposition. So much advice (some good, some bad) may be thrown at new teachers during their first few years that they need to take care not to become jaded or overwhelmed. They would also do well to distance themselves from the veteran complainers who may see all professional development opportunities as a waste of time. These are the teachers who have taught the same way for the past 25 years, haven't had a new idea or instructional strategy in that time, and can't understand why kids and new teachers today aren't "getting it." Coming out of years of classroom teaching, new mentors might think they are equipped with all the tools and knowledge they will ever need to mentor new teachers. Often they will find themselves sadly disappointed.

When new teachers hit the "wall of reality" in their first classroom, an experienced and informed mentor needs to be there. Effective and successful mentors quickly discover the benefits of seeking out professional development opportunities, formally and informally, to continually evaluate and strive to improve their practice.

Sources

McCotter, S. S. (2001). Collaborative groups as professional development. *Teaching and Teacher Education, 17*(6), 685–704.

McLaughlin, H. J. (1996). The nature and nurture of reflection. In K. Watson, C. Modgil, & S. Modgil (Eds.), *Teachers, teacher education and training* (p. 185). New York: Cassell.

 STRATEGY 3: Look at the mentoring process as more than a one-on-one relationship between mentor and beginning teacher.

What the Research Says

Since 1989, the state of Texas has experimented with mentoring for beginning teachers as a strategy to encourage and facilitate the retention of teachers. In 1990, the state created its alternative certification program, and mentoring was a required element for all alternatively certified teachers. In 1991, it was mandated for all teachers. In order to gain an understanding of the most current status of teacher mentoring activities in Texas school districts, researchers conducted a statewide survey that was sent to district superintendents during the spring of 2000. The data allowed the Southwest Educational Development Laboratory researchers to assess the scope, range of mentoring programs, mentoring activities, use of resources, and results. Data compiled represented 51% of all students in the state and 49% of all teachers. Responding districts reported student ethnic characteristics of 41% white, 41% Hispanic, 15% African American, and 3% other. Responding districts reported teacher ethnic characteristics of 72% white, 17% Hispanic, 10% African American and 1% other.

Two conditions that can contribute to first-year difficulties are the physical and social isolation that many new teachers experience (Lortie, 1975). This isolation varies but seems to be experienced more by new teachers in less effective schools. The Angelle study found that new teachers in less effective schools were more often forced to search for informal mentors for information and guidance involving all aspects of their professional responsibilities. In these situations they also labored to find their own resources, as few or none were voluntarily offered to them. In these less effective schools the main goals of the formal mentor were to "check" on the new teacher or observe and critique for assessment. There was little teaching, exchange, or sharing of relevant information or personal help given.

Application

It is critical for new teachers to surround themselves with exemplary experienced colleagues. In most schools, almost without exception, teachers work in settings where the sociocultural context, if not the actual physical structure, encourages little interaction among adults and can contribute to feelings of isolation and frustration. This can limit a new teacher's maturation and stifle professional growth.

A teacher's style is a very personal thing. Usually it is hard to find two alike on the same campus. Teachers are not made with a cookie cutter. As mentors develop an appropriate relationship with their new teachers, it is important to keep in mind that "style" is something that most people discover about themselves and is not something that is given to them. The mentors' job is not to create clones of their own instructional style; it is to help new teachers discover their own. The range of new teachers that are likely to be mentored may range from a 22 year old with no classroom experience to a reentry middle-aged change of career person who comes with very different life experiences. To mentor both at the same time, a mentor would not be able to treat them the same, as their needs vary.

In addition, what if the mentor's teaching philosophy differs from the new teacher's? What if the mentor starts to realize that the colleague next door seems to match the new teacher's instructional style better? Mentors have to be strong and confident enough to understand that new teachers need a variety of role models and professional contacts from which to draw ideas and inspiration.

New teachers benefit from the support of other teachers, administrators, and higher education partners. Induction mentoring is best developed within a professional culture that favors a collegial exchange of ideas. Egos can get in the way of this. Mentoring a new teacher can be a source of tremendous satisfaction that some may not want to share. Be ready to accept the idea that a colleague might upstage some ideas. However, it is up to the mentor to *help create and encourage* this type of collegial teaching and learning including facilitating a rich and varied supportive professional environment.

Precautions and Possible Pitfalls

 Sometimes the hardest thing for mentors to do is to not offer their opinions or to accept the idea that their solutions are not the only solutions. Sometimes it is better to offer the new teacher a range of options and solutions offering choice. This is a very different concept than telling them what the mentor would do.

Sources

Angelle, P. S. (2002). Mentoring the beginning teacher: Providing assistance in differentially effective middle schools. *The High School Journal* Oct/Nov, pp. 15–27.

Lortie, D. C. (1975). *Schoolteacher: A sociological study.* Chicago: University of Chicago Press.

Mutchler, S., Pan, D., Glover, R., & Shapley, K. (2000). Mentoring beginning teachers: Lessons from the experience in Texas. Southwest Educational Development Laboratory, Policy Research Report. http://www.sedl.org/pubs/policy23

 STRATEGY 4: *Encourage beginning teachers to look at conflict and tension as opportunities for personal growth and change.*

What the Research Says

New teachers vary in their ability to perceive, grapple with, and resolve the normal conflicts and tensions that exist in the teaching and classroom environments. As identified in the research (Beach & Pearson, 1998), some new teachers avoid or minimize conflicts and tensions by conforming to the system or authority figures in the workplace. Others are so overwhelmed that they find conflict and tension unmanageable, leading to a sense of loss of control, resignation, and futility or wanting escape from the system. A review of 16 studies (Beach & Pearson, 1998) on the effectiveness of programs fostering beginning teachers' reflections found that preservice and student teachers' reflections were primarily technical or practical, with little evidence of substantial reflection (Hatton & Smith, 1995). During early student teaching experiences, focus is usually concentrated on conflicts and tensions to developing basic teaching techniques. Later in student teaching and into their first year of teaching, teachers shift out of their more egocentric modes of teaching, learning, and relationships to focus more on their students and their students' reactions to their teaching. In this study (Beach & Pearson, 1998), 28 students enrolled in a 15-month postbaccalaureate teaching program were required to reflect on their clinical experiences in journals and small-group interactions.

Application

Four basic types of conflicts and tensions were categorized in Beach and Pearson's research that are useful to consider. These categories can be used in helping mentors more clearly define areas of concern and consideration in helping new teachers. They are:

1. Curriculum and instruction: conflicts and tensions between planned instruction and actual events or between teachers' perceptions and students' perceptions of relevancy, or beliefs about their own teaching and curricular choices and school- or department-mandated curriculum and pedagogy.

2. Interpersonal relationships: conflicts and tensions with and among students, other teaching colleagues, and administrators. This category could also relate to a sense of personal isolation.

3. Self-concept or role: personal conflicts and tensions regarding the need to be accepted and well liked, the role ambiguity of transition from student to teacher, and the further definition of self.

4. Contextual and institutional: conflicts and tensions related to the expectations of the institutions in which teachers work, teach, and learn. This generally involves acclimation and socialization to the culture of school and teaching.

The same research also identified three levels of strategies for coping with conflicts and tensions:

1. Avoidance/denial: In the beginning, new teachers frequently describe their dealings with conflicts and tensions in highly positive terms. Some assumed problems would diminish with time so they avoided coping.

2. Immediate solutions: New teachers frequently generate short-term, quick-fix solutions. They defer tensions and conflicts between the cooperating teachers or students to the back burner. They only deal with issues when they are forced to.

3. Incorporation: New teachers accept their conflicts and tensions as a necessary part of growth and incorporate positive changes and alteration of class and management structures to better avoid conflicts or create clear, workable mitigation plans for students. Informal professional support structures are created and integrated into interpersonal relationships with colleagues and administrators.

Most veteran teachers have developed their teaching and student interaction strategies to a point where most points of tension and conflicts are avoided. A veteran mentor can look at almost any situation and identify potential problems and help their new teachers read and anticipate situations and responses in advance. It's nice to prepare a new teacher with *answers* before there are *questions.* Mentors should use their intuition to benefit their new teachers.

Precautions and Possible Pitfalls

Good teaching is a continuous and exciting journey. If teachers think they will finally have it all down pat one day, they are mistaken. Unfortunately, it is still true that new teachers are often placed in a position of trial by fire. They are given assignments that more experienced teachers would never accept. It is common to have to teach in more than one room or teach a variety of classes, forcing the new teacher to prepare for multiple settings, disciplines, and ability levels. It is difficult to give advice for situations like this. In induction programs such as the Beginning Teacher Support and Assessment (BTSA) program in California, there is support for new teachers to limit the number of preparations, classroom changes, and involvement on multiple committees and coaching assignments through the first two years. It is ironic that the most inexperienced teachers are often given the most challenging assignments. Good planning and communication with all stakeholders help.

Sources

Beach, R., & Pearson, D. (1998). Changes in preservice teachers' perceptions of conflict and tension. *Teaching and Teacher Education, 14*(3), 337–351.

Hatton, N., & Smith, D. (1995). Reflection in teacher education: Towards definition and implementation. *Teaching and Teacher Education, 11*(10), 33–49.

STRATEGY 5: *Use site politics as an induction topic and a consideration in mentored relationships.*

What the Research Says

Beyond classroom and student issues, there are a number of hidden beginning teacher acclimation challenges. Professional socialization within a school is one of these. Socialization beyond the classroom was the focus of this study. Researchers describe the term *praxis shock* as the new teachers' confrontation with the realities and responsibilities of being classroom teachers. The shock comes when they implement their beliefs and ideas about teaching in a real classroom. The classroom environment often challenges many of them and confirms others.

In this study, information was collected from 14 beginning teachers in Flemish primary schools with a minimum of 3 years experience and a maximum of 5 years experience. The data collected attempted to answer questions on how beginning teachers experience their professional socialization during their induction phase. Further, researchers looked into how beginning teachers confronted the micropolitical realities of schools during their professional socialization/induction.

Researchers described socialization as the beginning teachers' self-interest in

- Looking for self-affirmation or self-confidence
- Coping with vulnerability
- Coping with visibility

Essentially, the study found that teachers needed to feel successful both inside and outside the classroom for successful development of self-confidence and a positive socially recognized identity. If their social recognition is threatened by hitting their own professional limits, they feel threatened and vulnerable. This vulnerability is further increased by their high degree of visibility as new teachers within the school social structure. Visibility is particularly high, with frequent visits by other teachers, contact with parents, and contact with older students. Almost every teacher in the study strongly emphasized the importance of good relationships with other members of the school.

Application

 The research clarified and put words to the self-evident presence of the micropolitical dimension of teacher induction. For the mentor, it points to the task of helping new teachers become more micropolitically aware, active, and helping them develop some micropolitical literacy within their new teachers. Mentors can help new teachers move from a reactive to proactive mode. Reactive strategies should be aimed at maintaining a safe learning environment or protecting the teacher from certain conditions. Proactive strategies are directed toward changing the situation or influencing the conditions, helping the new teacher anticipate problems, and developing solutions before they are needed.

Micropolitical action can take many very different forms in the reality of the social context. The analysis stresses that the goal of understanding micropolitics is learning to read situations and conditions through a professional eye. This involves understanding them in terms of stakeholders and interests and being able to deal, cope, or avoid them as necessary. Ultimately a new teacher will be able to develop micropolitical strategies and tactics in order to establish, safeguard, or restore their own work environment. Micropolitical reality for new teachers often triggers intense emotional discomfort, uncertainty, powerlessness, and sometimes anger. A mentor can turn struggle and conflict into collaboration and coalition building, replacing insecurities with meaningful interactions between a new teacher and the professional context.

Veteran teachers and mentor teachers usually know those in the school setting who have the formal and informal power to affect a teacher's working conditions. They also know how to get things done and avoid pitfalls and time wasting. They know the community, the administration, and how to develop and maintain political standing and currency. Some of this micropolitical literacy can only be learned by experience and some can be taught. A savvy mentor will know whether experience (with reflection) or direct early mentoring is the best strategy for learning professional socialization skills.

What is clear is that micropolitical literacy is an important issue in the induction phase of teaching. It is difficult for many teachers to understand the complexities of the workplace outside of the classroom and can significantly influence the next career stages.

Precautions and Possible Pitfalls

The cost of not alerting new teachers to the most effective ways to get things done outside the classroom can be huge. Parents, students, and others within the school environment can ambush new teachers with problems they are not prepared for. The school bureau-cracy can drain confidence and foster insecurity. This is especially true with class management and discipline issues. All teachers want the support of assistant principals regarding discipline problems. Teachers want protection from aggressive parents and misbehaving students. Most new teachers fear calling attention to their discipline problems for fear it will reflect on their teaching. They need to learn when to call for help and how to utilize the support avenues available to them. There are times in class management when problems need to be transferred to others once the teacher's system fails to obtain the desired changes. Mentors need to support their teachers in identifying these points and optional supporting pathways. Should the problem be a counseling or assistant principal issue? When should the teacher alert the administration to a possible parent call or complaint? How can a new teacher be professional, proactive, and effective in these situations? Mentors should have these answers thought out ahead of time in anticipation of needing options for their new teachers.

Sources

Kelchtermans, G., & Ballet, K. (2002). The micro politics of teacher induction: A narrative-biographical study on teacher socialization. *Teaching and Teacher Education, 18*, 105–120.

Orland, L. (2001). Reading a mentoring situation: One aspect of learning to mentor. *Teaching and Teacher Education, 17*, 75–88.

> **STRATEGY 6:** *Mentally prepare for special challenges such as late hires to the school or new teachers taking over classes mid-year.*

What the Research Says

 In order to gain an understanding of the most current status of teacher mentoring activities in Texas school districts, researchers conducted a statewide survey that was sent to district superintendents during the spring of 2000. These data allowed the Southwest Educational Development Laboratory researchers to assess the scope and range of mentoring programs, mentoring activities, use of resources, and results. In the final chapter of their research, the authors made specific recommendations and identified a number of challenges from mentors. The following application addresses one of the major challenges faced by mentors as identified in their research: new teachers coming into schools and classrooms out of sequence with a September starting time.

Application

Coming to an assignment late or in the middle of a term presents mentors with special problems. The new teacher is likely to be especially needy. Ideally, new teachers have enough time to develop their own "best" guess for appropriate curriculum and instructional development within their level of expertise and ability. Coming to a school late or taking over a class midterm cuts out this important mental and collaborative acclimation time. A mentor can be especially helpful here in "scaffolding" support based on the needs of the new teacher and that teacher's assignment. The research identified these three scenarios as creating the most concern:

- Teachers asked to use unique or innovative instructional approaches in which the new teacher has no background
- The assignment of a new teacher to a subject or a grade level in which he or she has no experience or field preparation
- The presence of many new teachers, all of whom need some degree of mentoring

Ideally, in situations such as these and a few others, the mentor will want to move the teacher from day-to-day survival mode to more long-term planning as quickly as possible. The most common expression of novice teachers who are facing their own classes for the first time is "feeling overwhelmed" by their students, by lesson planning, by new responsibilities, by paperwork, and more. What can be done?

Lesson planning is the most obvious way to reduce stress. If the mentor or another colleague is teaching the same class, have the new teacher "piggy back" curriculum, lessons, and activities. This would not necessarily deprive a new teacher of the opportunity to develop planning skills; however, in an emergency it may be required. If the piggy backing can't be done, there might be some interim steps to take to help minimize the curriculum and instructional void. Most departments have some tried and true strategies that have been shared by teachers in the department. The more familiar the material and the situation, the more comfortable the students and the parents will be.

Second, veteran students at any school can make life very hard for new teachers, long-term subs, or replacement teachers. If the mentor is a respected veteran teacher and a mentor, he or she can help the new teacher by his or her association with the new teacher in front of the students. If the students see new teachers as part of the school team, they are less likely to view them as outsiders.

Class management is hard enough for veterans. By visiting new teachers' rooms during class, participating in team teaching, or offering some other types of visible support, mentors can help integrate new teachers into the school and department fabric. Remember, most new teachers are good with content, but class management and discipline always offer the greatest challenge. They may have a plan, but veteran teachers know that as soon as the plan is articulated, the students will test it. New teachers feel the dilemma between being liked and maintaining discipline. Mentors know the school, the kids, and the general school behavior standards. They can help tremendously here by providing detailed help when student behavior and discipline become ambiguous for the new teacher. The simple act of looking over a class roster for potential "red flag" students can be a proactive rather than a reactive step in class management.

Also, every school has a discipline pattern between the classroom teacher and the administration. Familiarizing the new teacher with the management and discipline culture of the school can help acclimate the new teacher.

The bottom line is that mentoring is not always as clean as would be hoped. Mentors may be asked to respond to a less than ideal mentoring situation. By thinking about these issues ahead of time they can avoid some of the pitfalls of late planning. Ultimately, the students will benefit and everyone will feel more in control and empowered.

Precautions and Possible Pitfalls

 Mentors shouldn't assume things are all right because they don't hear from the new teachers. Time is a key here. Mentor–new teacher relationships are built during time together. Mentors may have a situation where new teachers don't ask for help for a number of reasons. Mentors should be careful not to let their opportunity to succeed slip away because new teachers don't ask for help. Mentors may have to be the leaders here and create space for time together whether new teachers ask for help or not.

Source

Mutchler, S., Pan, D., Glover, R., & Shapley, K. (2000). *Mentoring beginning teachers: Lessons from the experience in Texas.* Southwest Educational Development Laboratory, Policy Research Report. http://www.sedl.org/pubs/policy23.

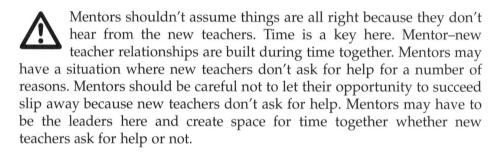

STRATEGY 7: Be aware that beginning teachers in less effective schools are at greater risk for leaving the field than those teaching at more effective schools.

What the Research Says

 This study was designed to answer the question, does the socialization experience of beginning teachers placed in effective schools vary from those placed in less effective schools? To add to this, what are the processes effective in schools that account for these differences? And finally, what role does mentoring assistance play in the beginning socialization experience? The study took place in Louisiana and focused on middle schools. The terms and "profiles" of effective and noneffective schools were determined using a school effectiveness index covering many variables typical of school operation. Test scores, attendance, drop out rates, and other factors were included in the determination. In this study, *beginning teacher* refers to one who had less than three years of total experience.

It was found that less effective schools breed less effectiveness and more effective schools breed greater effectiveness, with inertia maintaining the status quo. Principals, mentors, and naïve beginning teachers did not set out to lead poorly, mentor poorly, or teach poorly, but the researchers found that the "health" or "illness" of the school culture transferred that health or illness to the community members who worked and taught there. It was found that the healthy atmosphere or the sick building syndrome had a direct impact on the socialization experiences of these beginning teachers and transferred to their intention to remain in the field of teaching.

Application

 The results of the study speak volumes on the socialization experience from good mentoring (in more effective schools) and bad mentoring (in less effective schools) perspectives. Here are the characteristics typically found in both placements as described in this research.

Mentoring Characteristics in Less Effective Schools

- In less effective schools, new teachers were forced to seek out guidance and informal mentoring for procedures regarding day-to-day activities, knowledge of planning, paperwork, curriculum, and classroom management.
- Teachers were offered few resources and had to find their own.
- The activity of the mentor was largely limited to checking, editing, or rechecking the lesson plans or making critiques and observations.

Mentoring Characteristics in More Effective Schools

- Schools promoted mentoring from the whole person perspective.
- Mentors in more effective schools were proactive.
- The mentor took the lead in providing information ahead of time and worked with the new teachers much like an aide helping with paperwork.
- Mentors role-played as parents with the new teacher prior to conferences.
- Mentors role-played student management and discipline scenarios.
- Mentors met frequently with new teachers and sought them out rather than waiting for them.
- The principal's expectations for the mentors were that their role was a vital one.
- Mentors focused on the assimilation of their new teachers into the total school culture.

Individual mentoring perspectives depend on how mentors see their school. Regardless of how the school is classified, the key to effective assistance is in the extent of the support provided. Even in under-performing schools there are generally pockets of good teachers to draw mentors from. Mentors who find themselves in a less effective school may want to develop their mentoring skills to compensate for weaknesses in other parts of the school's environment. The sooner new teachers feel in control of their environment, the happier they will be. Merely providing support in order to fill the state mandated assessment was the norm in less effective schools.

Highlighting another important point, it was found that mentors at less effective schools were more likely to relate concerns about conflicts with their mentoring and be less than optimistic about teaching in general. Mentoring tended to fall low on their priority list behind their other duties. Full-time teaching loads were cited more often as a problem in providing mentoring. Administrative expectations for the mentors in less effective schools were cited as being limited to recommending or not recommending certification as the ultimate goal.

Precautions and Possible Pitfalls

In districts or schools that have no mentor training or formal expectations it is up to individual mentors to decide what they are willing to do. Mentors shouldn't rely on their own personal student teaching or new teacher induction experiences to serve as a mentor model (unless it was a really good experience). There are many proven models and guidelines out there. Mentors should seek them out and learn what they can add to their own vision and what already works for them.

Sources

Angelle, P. (2002). Mentoring the beginning teacher: Providing assistance in differentially effective middle schools. *High School Journal, V86, iL,* 15–28.

Orland, L. (2001). Reading a mentoring situation: One aspect of learning to mentor. *Teaching and Teacher Education, 17,* 75–88.

 STRATEGY 8: *Integrate the principal into the induction loop as a key source of support and guidance for the beginning teacher.*

What the Research Says

The purpose of this study was to examine the perceptions of principals and beginning teachers regarding problems, role expectations, and assistance in the first year of teaching. The researchers wanted to discover what differences existed from each unique perspective about assistance first-year teachers wanted and what principals were willing to provide. Seventy-five elementary and high school teachers were surveyed at the beginning of their second teaching year. Forty-nine returned the survey. During the second stage, 75 principals were surveyed, with 46 returning surveys on their expectations for beginning teachers and the problems teachers encountered during their first year. This survey also included a look at what principals thought the components and methods of the first-year induction program should be.

Application

The expectations of the new teachers in this study clearly illustrate that principals are seen as central to the successful socialization and first-year induction of beginning teachers. Although much of the literature and research deals with mentor or teacher-to-teacher relationships, it is clear that principals are key figures in the eyes of the first-year teacher. Ultimately, it is usually the principal who holds the new teacher's fate in his or her hands. The principal decides if the new teacher is worth fighting to retain. Ultimately the principal also recommends upgrading a teacher from temporary to probationary or probationary to tenure. If the new teacher moves on, it is the principal who will write the letter of recommendation or make an important telephone call.

Within the research, the principals reported that their first-year teachers should be able to demonstrate the following proficiencies:

- A professional attitude
- Adequate knowledge of the subject area
- Good classroom management skills
- Excellent communication skills
- A belief that every child can learn
- A desire to help students succeed

The beginning teachers listed a variety of expectations that they had for the principals.

- They wanted principals to clearly communicate the prevailing criteria for good teaching and lesson plans.
- They wanted principals to explain what to expect and what the principal's role was.
- They wanted to be introduced to the entire staff, not just other teachers.
- They wanted classroom visits, feedback, and affirmation.
- They wanted to meet and discuss the culture, traditions, and history of the school.

The first principal in a teacher's career usually holds a special place in the minds of new teachers. The teacher may move on, or the principal might change, but the first one is the one who new teachers negotiate with first for professional working status. In many cases it's the first principal who influences a new teacher's career the most. They have a big say in what comes next for the new teacher. In the social structure of schools, the principal holds the keys to the resources and the teaching assignments and the power to make things happen. In contrast to new teachers, the power structure is just not the same for veteran teachers. Research on the subject is difficult to find, but principals seem to relate to those they hire differently (usually more favorably) than to those they inherit from their schools.

The principal plays a major role for new teachers in the first 3 to 5 years. If mentors believe in their new teachers, it is their job to facilitate a relationship between the new teacher and the principal. This is especially true if there is no more formalized contact between the principal and the new teacher in the school's induction process.

Precautions and Possible Pitfalls

 Some mentors have egos that demand the full attention of their new teachers. They want to be the sole expert in their new teachers' lives. They are reluctant to involve others in the induction loop for fear of "competition" with others that may conflict with the mentor's relationship with the new teacher. Diverse opinion is a good thing. Mentors should refer new teachers to others if they offer something special or something they are really good at doing. Mentors should observe the work of teachers respected on staff. Mentors should introduce new teachers to the school's best special education teacher and counselor so when they need advice they know who to go to. New teachers need to know who can meet their needs in the office and within the nonteaching staff.

Source

Brock, B., & Grady, M. (1998). Beginning teacher induction programs: The role of the principal. *Clearing House, 71*(3), 179–184.

STRATEGY 9: *Use job sharing arrangements to produce personal and supportive "co- or peer mentoring" relationships within the learning environment.*

What the Research Says

 This article provides a narrative describing the fifth year (first year of teaching) induction experience of two middle school science teachers as partners in a job sharing arrangement. The writers tell the story of their shared experiences as first-year teachers in the Southeastern United States. In their state, student teachers are allowed to accept paid teaching positions if they are enrolled in and remain enrolled in a fifth-year teaching program at a college or university. The two new teachers shared a middle school science assignment (one taught two integrated science classes and the other taught three). At their site, they were officially "mentored" by an assistant principal and "supported" by the department's lead teacher. In reality, mutual mentoring or peer mentoring by each other replaced a more typical mentoring arrangement, and the assistant principal served as an assessment mentor assuming responsibility for their formal first-year evaluations. The department lead teacher helped them with questions and issues they couldn't solve themselves, most importantly those to improve their classroom discipline.

Both women supported a philosophy of a hands-on and inquiry-based instruction strategy that was in line with the "student-centered" approach favored by the school administration (but not by all teachers at the school). The two teachers were compatible with each other for nonevaluative support through regular dialog with each other and as familiar, respected, and trusted colleagues. Their shared philosophy helped them develop a productive "co- or peer mentoring" environment to buffer the sink or swim situation that existed for others at the school. The study showed how job sharing and peer mentoring, in the absence of a true induction program, could facilitate the induction of new teachers or student teachers.

The researcher (Eick, 2002) pointed out that while peer mentoring was productive in this case, these teachers could have benefited by more time with an experienced mentor or pairing with a second- or third-year teacher.

Application

While not directly a mentor strategy, creative educators dealing with induction could discover a model for new teacher success within this research. There are a variety and range of induction programs, student teaching, and preservice teaching arrangements throughout the nation's schools. Some are very formal and structured and others are very fluid and informal. Every district and school conducts the business of teacher induction differently. Eick's research model will not be for everyone, but it could be the answer for successful induction in some settings. The model could also be modified to fit the individual needs of a specific school or district.

Imagine pairing new teachers with a part-time veteran to fill a full time vacancy. This could benefit the new teacher and the person responsible for the master schedule. Pairing two student teachers would relieve the tension of a single assignment and offer them an instant collaborator usually long before the first day of school. For a master teacher or teacher-mentor, pairing two student teachers could help buffer the isolation and emotional needs of both teachers and free the mentor to focus on specific issues both teachers share.

While the cited model isn't for everyone, it does foster "out of the box" thinking regarding mentor–student teacher–new teacher arrangements. While teaching partnerships are generally rare, in this case it did foster collegiality and sharing of the student teacher experience. The classrooms of beginning teachers are fast paced and filled with surprises. Working with a partner slows the pace and helps level the ups and downs of that first assignment. Daily observation, dialogue, and reflection on practice increased the depth of their involvement. Their job sharing arrangement provided many supports that are not available to struggling beginning teachers going it alone. Finally, these types of relationships do facilitate and model the sort of collegiality that helps even the most veteran teachers in their careers from time to time.

Precautions and Possible Pitfalls

As with any "group work" in the classroom, educational mismatches in many areas can pop up. Student teaching and first-year teaching are filled with drama about right career choices, knowledge and experience, commitment, and life changes in general. It is easy to see thata mismatch could create as many problems as solutions, and careful screening of potential partners is important. A quick call to a college or university contact or other reference could help avoid these pitfalls.

Source

Eick, C. J. (2002). Job sharing their first year: A narrative of two partnered teachers' induction into middle school science teaching. *Teacher and Teacher Education, 18*, 887–904.

2

Supporting New Teachers as They Interact and Collaborate With Students

Individual commitment to a group effort—that is what makes a team work, a company work, a society work, a civilization work.

Vince Lombardi

Everyone who remembers his own educational experience remembers teachers, not methods and techniques.

Sidney Hook

 STRATEGY 10: *Encourage beginning teachers to think about homework from the perspective of students.*

What the Research Says

 A recent book by John Buell and Etta Kralovec presents a unique view of the homework concept and questions the value of the practice itself. Few studies have been conducted on the subject, and while the book offers perspectives from both sides of the debate, it is clear that the homework concept needs to be examined more closely. For example, Buell and Kralovec cite homework as a great discriminator, as children, once leaving school for the day, encounter a range of parental supports, challenging home environments, after-school jobs and sports, and a mix of resources available to some and not to others. Clearly, opportunities are not equal. Tired parents are held captive by the demands of their children's school, unable to develop their own priorities for family life.

Buell and Kralovec also provide examples of communities that have tried to formalize homework policy as the communities tried to balance the demands of homework with extracurricular activities and the need for family time. They also point out the aspects of inequity inherent in the fact that many students lack the resources at home to compete on equal footing with those peers who have computers, Internet access, highly educated parents, and unlimited funds and other resources for homework requirements.

They also point out that homework persists despite the lack of any solid evidence that it achieves its much-touted gains. Homework is one of our most entrenched institutional practices, yet one of the least investigated.

The questions Buell and Kralovec's research and discourse explore are "With single parent households becoming more common, or with both parents working, is it reasonable to accept the homework concept, as it is now practiced, as useful and valid considering the tradeoffs families need to make?" "How does homework contribute to family dynamics in negative or positive ways?" "Does it unnecessarily stifle other important opportunities or create an uneven or unequal playing field for some students?"

Applications

Frequently a new teacher has no concept of too much or too little when it comes to homework. A mentor can discuss with a new teacher a variety of questions taking into consideration any school or district philosophy or policy regarding homework. New teachers working with their mentors should be aware of the inequalities that may exist within the range of students in their classes regarding their ability to complete homework assignments. Certain students may be excluded from the opportunities for support and other resources. Consider the following questions:

- What is homework?
- How much homework is too much?

- What are or should be the purposes of homework?
- Can different assignments be given to different students in the same class?
- Do all your students have equal opportunity to successfully complete the homework?
- Who is responsible for homework, the students or the parents?
- Do all your students have the same capacity to self-regulate?
- How are other school activities or family-based responsibilities factored in?
- What is the best and most equable way to deal with overachievers?
- Is the homework load balanced between teachers?

Precautions and Possible Pitfalls

 Traditionally, homework has been seen as a solution rather than the cause of educational problems. It takes a little bit of acclimation time to begin to look at the homework concept with new eyes. However, the value of homework in providing opportunities for students to deepen their science knowledge should not be ignored. This is especially important for students in the United States, whose achievement lags behind students from other countries that have longer school days and years. Beware the politics involved in any discourse regarding the homework concept. For example, if a teacher doesn't give any homework but the rest of the department does, it may create some conflict. New teachers should be reminded that students often discuss workload among themselves, and this may contribute to teacher reputation of "too hard" or "too easy."

Source

Buell, J., & Kralovec, E. (2000). *The end of homework: How homework disrupts families, overburdens children, and limits learning.* Boston: Beacon.

 STRATEGY 11: Encourage beginning teachers to add humor to student interactions.

What the Research Says

 When students are asked to describe exemplary teachers, one of the essential characteristics they choose is a sense of humor. Students frequently recall that their favorite teachers made them laugh and, more important, made learning fun. Glasser (1986) includes fun in his list of the five primary needs of humans, along with survival, belonging, power, and freedom. He further asserts that all behavior is a constant attempt to satisfy one or more of those needs. It is no secret that teachers who engage students have found the use of humor as a positive way of putting students at ease, gaining attention, and showing students that the teacher is indeed human.

According to Quina (1989), if teachers and students can laugh together, they can most likely work together as well. In these days of standards and high-stakes accountability, if students are comfortable and enjoy the learning process, they are more likely to remember more of the material presented.

Csikzentmihalyi and McCormack (1995) indicate that only after a student has learned to love learning does education truly begin. What student doesn't reflect fondly on a teacher who used stories, analogies, or amusing anecdotes to enhance learning and aid in the retention of knowledge?

Application

Mentors can use humor with a new teacher to help break the ice, provide an inviting classroom or collegial climate, and establish an easy, comfortable relationship. In turn, mentors should give feedback to new teachers on appropriate use of humor from their classroom observations. Mentors would do well to remind new teachers that humor does not simply mean telling jokes. Humor involves putting a positive spin on reality. Humor should never be used in a negative way, which involves sarcasm or cynicism. Teachers and mentors who use humor in positive ways model a better way to deal with everyday, adverse situations; and it teaches new teachers and students not to take small crises or bumps in the road too seriously.

In addition, humor helps teachers deal with the stress of teaching, whether one is a first-year teacher or a seasoned veteran. It can stimulate creative and flexible thinking, facilitate learning, and improve interest and attention in the classroom.

Humor can be an extremely useful tool in building rapport. Teachers who can laugh at themselves and can laugh with (but never at) students can help establish a positive, inviting classroom climate.

Mentors can also suggest how the use of humor can do a lot to generate interest and grab a reluctant student's attention. The teacher who dresses up as Abraham Lincoln to deliver the Gettysburg Address or writes and performs a rap song to learn the endocrine system and its functions will make the information presented memorable for the students.

One of the many characteristics of a good teacher is to aid students as they become active learners. A goal of many teachers is to have students enjoy not only the class but also the subject matter. The appropriate use of humor can help achieve this goal.

The feedback given new teachers by mentors can help new teachers to discover whether or not they are trying too hard, whether the humor is appropriate to the age group, and if the teacher is coming off as humorous or seen by the students as trying too hard to be funny.

Precautions and Possible Pitfalls

A teacher must always be careful not to use inappropriate humor that could be offensive, sarcastic, or that makes references to ethnic, racial, religious, or gender differences. This type of humor is totally inappropriate in the classroom and is almost always at the expense of students. All teachers must be sensitive to cultural differences and not assume that all students will find their use of humor funny. Sometimes teachers can try too hard to be funny and joke around with their students. Teachers may see themselves as cool and being "with it," while the students may find their teachers' use of humor as "lame" or "corny." This is an area in which the mentor can give feedback to new teachers based on classroom observations.

It is important for each teacher to find the type of humor he or she is comfortable with using. A teacher can start slowly by reading a funny quip or quotation. A teacher could share a particularly corny joke at the start or end of each class session, thereby beginning a class tradition. Mentors can also direct new teachers to observe exemplary teachers whose use of humor is appropriate and enhances student learning. One veteran teacher observed broke the tension before a midterm exam by putting the following on an overhead transparency just before tests were distributed: "As long as teachers give tests . . . there will be prayer in school."

Sources

Csikzentmihalyi, M., & McCormack, J. (1995). The influence of teachers. In K. Ryan & J. Cooper (Eds.), *Kaleidoscope: Readings in education* (pp. 2–8). Boston: Houghton Mifflin.

Glasser, W. (1986). *Control theory in the classroom.* New York: Harper & Row.

Quina, J. (1989). Effective secondary teaching: Going beyond the bell curve. New York: Harper & Row.

 STRATEGY 12: Show beginning teachers how to lighten their own loads by training students to be tutors.

What the Research Says

A classroom of students helping other students has been found to be an efficient and effective method of enhancing achievement. Twenty teachers participated in a study of classwide peer tutoring with 40 classrooms in elementary and middle schools. Half of the schools implemented classwide peer tutoring programs and half did not. Both urban and suburban schools participated in the study. Students came from diverse backgrounds, both culturally and linguistically. There were three categories of students: average achievers, low achievers without learning disabilities, and low achievers with learning disabilities. The peer tutoring programs were conducted 3 days a week, 35 minutes a day, for 15 weeks. Stronger students were paired with weaker students. Teachers reviewed each pair to ensure they were socially compatible. In all pairs, students took turns serving in the roles of tutor and tutee. Student pairs worked together for four weeks; then teachers arranged new pairings. Teachers received training on how to train their students to be tutors. Tutor training included teaching students how to correct each other's errors. Achievement tests were administered before and after the peer tutoring program. Regardless of whether students were average achievers or low achievers, with or without learning disabilities, students in the peer tutoring classrooms achieved higher levels than those in the classrooms without classwide peer tutoring.

Application

For a new teacher in a new school, the opinion and help of a veteran teacher-mentor are essential in implementing this strategy. There are many areas in all content classes that lend themselves to a peer tutoring program. When there is a skill to be learned and all one needs is experience with success (i.e., drill with immediate feedback), then peer tutoring could provide an efficient way to monitor and support a student trying to master the skill. Say a student has difficulty with a specialized task and it becomes a sticking point in a larger activity. Individual students within groups can specialize as peer tutors in their specialty or act as a general peer tutor (under the guidance of a teacher). This can be quite beneficial for all involved. There are many tests at which peer tutors can become expert and then share their expertise with individual students. A student who has difficulty doing these tests could find that a peer tutor is a genuine asset.

Foreign-language classes are a natural for tutoring. Advanced students can routinely help less-skilled language students. Rather than waiting for an opportunity to talk with the teacher, a student has access to the peer tutor, saving everyone time. Additionally, in explaining the methodology to the student, the tutor is also provided with an opportunity to strengthen his or her own understanding of the concept of test reactions or a specific element of language (a higher-order thinking skill). Thus, there is often a mutual benefit to a peer tutoring program.

A mentor can help a new teacher identify specific students or classes that can be trusted or benefit from this strategy. Without a veteran teacher's support, this strategy's success rate would be reduced or it could be turned into a disaster. However, under the right circumstances this strategy could mean the difference between the success or failure of an activity for a new teacher.

Precautions and Possible Pitfalls

Teachers need to know that not every student makes a good tutor. Some are not mature enough to manage the responsibility. A tutor-training program offered by the teacher can precede peer tutoring. Some students are natural tutors, while some must be given instruction on how to conduct the specific concepts or sessions, what sort of difficulties to look for on the part of the tutee, and what points to stress in the sessions (based on the teacher's assessment of the class). Any individual difficulties on the part of the tutees should be mentioned to the tutor prior to the sessions. Tutors should be taught to guide student learning and *not* merely solve problems for students. Students with severe learning disabilities may not be receptive to tutoring or benefit from classwide peer tutoring, unless the tutors first receive individualized instruction from learning disability specialists.

Finally, there may be classes in which a tutoring system simply doesn't fit. Classes with discipline problems or classes with homogeneous learners may not provide the best setting to begin a tutoring program. In some cases managing tutors in tough classes can be more trouble than it is worth. The mentor should carefully consider the new teacher and the class before committing to this method.

Source

Fuchs, D., Fuchs, L., Mathes, P. G., & Simmons, D. (1997). Peer-assisted learning strategies: Making classrooms more responsive to diversity. *American Educational Research Journal, 34*(1), 174–206.

STRATEGY 13: Help beginning teachers and student teachers understand the full range of the nonacademic (just growing up) curriculum students bring into their classrooms.

What the Research Says

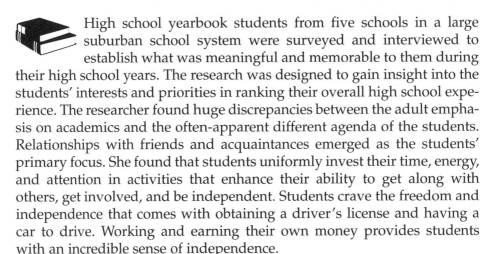 High school yearbook students from five schools in a large suburban school system were surveyed and interviewed to establish what was meaningful and memorable to them during their high school years. The research was designed to gain insight into the students' interests and priorities in ranking their overall high school experience. The researcher found huge discrepancies between the adult emphasis on academics and the often-apparent different agenda of the students. Relationships with friends and acquaintances emerged as the students' primary focus. She found that students uniformly invest their time, energy, and attention in activities that enhance their ability to get along with others, get involved, and be independent. Students crave the freedom and independence that comes with obtaining a driver's license and having a car to drive. Working and earning their own money provides students with an incredible sense of independence.

Students demonstrated a lack interest or importance in academics based on the minimal coverage academics received in their yearbooks and yearbook classes. Academics clashed with their personal priorities. The importance of ethos and rites of passage and social maturation were deemed priorities. Overall, students demonstrate an awareness of high school as a four-year rite-of-passage experience over the more adult notion of school for academics.

Application

The research tells us that most students are primarily engaged in the work of growing up. They value experiences that encourage and support their efforts to be involved, to get along with everyone, and to develop independence. Most new teachers mistakenly immerse themselves in academic goals and objectives, their content, and what they are going to teach. They forget their own memories of high school priorities and often show little empathy to rite of passage issues or the social maturation of their students. These clash with their traditional goals for their students. They wonder what's happening to their classrooms the week before the prom or homecoming. How can they rally support for their lessons the week after winter or spring break? Relationship breakups often lead to weeks of academic disinterest by seemingly good students. Jobs and sports rob some students of homework time. Puberty issues can also create havoc in a young student's life. All these things and more often leave young teachers wondering where their students' academic interests went.

Mentors can help their teachers comprehend these issues, thus explaining away seemingly strange behavior within certain individual students or their classes. Once a new teacher is able to show some empathy and understanding, some of the mystery of rites of passage and social maturation issues will disappear. New teachers can begin to become more proactive in reducing the classroom trauma to their academic goals and objectives. Developing a sense of timing is important in knowing when to push and when to lighten up.

New teachers also need to develop a sense of their own comfort levels in how far they want or need to explore their students' lives outside of purely academic areas. Often a few words of interest or understanding will provide a teacher with enough personal insight to help students regain their academic equilibrium. Awareness will also help new teachers design experiences that encourage and support their students' efforts to be involved, to get along with everyone, and to develop independence. If they are able to see school through their students' eyes, essential "adolescent ethos" elements can be recognized and understood rather than ignored, suppressed, or worked around. Teachers can look in a yearbook to see what is important to students. Restructuring and reform efforts rarely incorporate what students think are important in their lives. Mentors can play an important role in helping new teachers build awareness of these issues into their overall teaching toolbox.

Alert the new teacher to typical behaviors involving rite of passage events within the school's calendar. Each age group also comes with some typical predictable characteristics. These can be shared. Encourage new teachers to share curious student behaviors or sudden changes in student performance. Mutual reflection can often explain potential problems or help teachers develop strategies in mitigating rite of passage problems.

Precautions and Possible Pitfalls

Occasionally teachers get too involved in their students' lives, and the line between a teacher's role and a student's personal life begins to blur. Empathy is a great quality, but it can be taken too far. A teacher's inquiry into the personal life of a student can easily be misunderstood and create parental concern. A mentor can also role-play a scenario with a new teacher, pointing out potential pitfalls in strategies.

Sources

Hoffman, L. M. (2002). Why high schools don't change: What students and their yearbooks tell us. *High School Journal, 86,* 22–38.

Hoffman, L. M. (2002). What students need in a restructured high school. *Education Week, 22*(7), 34–38.

STRATEGY 14: Help beginning teachers understand the factors that foster the avoidance of "help-seeking behavior" in the classroom.

What the Research Says

Help seeking is an important self-regulatory strategy and survival skill that contributes to student learning and successful teaching. Most, if not all, students encounter miscommunication, ambiguity, or difficulty in their schoolwork and need assistance. In these situations savvy students need to adopt compensatory behavior. Usually they develop strategies for seeking the necessary help. This occurs as students become older and their metacognitive skills improve and they are better able to monitor and reflect on their performance and to determine their need for help in an academic situation. However, many mature adolescents do not seek help with their academic work.

Often there is a contradiction between this cognitive development and their help-seeking behavior. This study investigated the motivational and social factors that influence help-seeking behavior. Researchers used the term *avoidance of help seeking* to refer to instances when students know they need help but do not seek it. Using this theme, researchers did literature reviews finding "student seeking help avoidance" related studies. They then discussed their work regarding perceptions of academic and social competence and achievement and social-goal orientations. From there they explored the classroom-related context related to student help-seeking avoidance and decision to avoid asking for help.

They identified several reasons why students avoid asking for help in the classroom:

- It may not be practical or feasible during class.
- There may be explicit rules or norms against help seeking.
- Students may judge that asking for help is not going to be effective because there is not a competent or willing helper.
- It will take too long to get help.
- Two psychosocial concerns are a desire for autonomy (I can do it by myself) and to be seen as capable. The need for help is often construed as an indicator that one lacks competency.
- Seeking help may be evidence of a lack of ability.
- Help seekers are afraid of a negative reaction or judgment from others (both teachers and other students/peers).

Researchers found that in academic settings the need for help is most threatening to low-achieving students and those with low self-esteem or low perceptions of cognitive competence. In contrast, students who are high achievers or who have high cognitive perceptions are less likely to worry that others will attribute help seeking as a lack of ability. Feeling comfortable and skillful in relating to others (socially competent) lessens the perceptions and fears of negative reactions or judgments from others.

Researchers also identified achievement-goal orientations grouped around help seeking. The first concerned mastery goals, the focus on learning and self-improvement. The second concerned performance goals such as trying to compete or race against others or gaining public recognition for superior performance. These two orientations put help seeking into two contexts and come from two motivational perspectives. The second orientation relates to social achievement, in contrast to academic achievement in the first. Social behavior in the classroom is usually connected to social achievement as well as academic achievement. Group membership, visibility, and prestige are grouped into social status goals. The sense of self-relating (self-worth) to others heightens the tension, and help seeking (or not seeking help) is a public behavior that has the potential to garner attention from one's peers. This can be threatening to students' self-worth. Seeking help or not seeking help within the classroom then becomes an opportunity for peer interaction. Social motivational constructs and academic achievement are both than associated and linked to help seeking behavior.

Application

It is very important to help facilitate an awareness of the factors associated with helping seeking. The goal of all teachers is to design classroom environments in which students who need help ask for it. When students do not ask for help when they need it, they run the risk of undermining their learning and academic achievement. From a mentoring perspective, many new teachers are often more concerned about their own performance than the performance of their students. Some students quickly find subtle ways to discourage teachers from trying to include them in class activities, answering questions, or class discussions. It is only after teachers become comfortable with themselves as teachers that they can decentralize and transfer their concerns to these students and to their learning issues.

The classroom structure is communicated to students in many ways. The social nature of help seeking makes the social climate of the classroom an important consideration in influencing help-seeking behavior. A mastery-goal structure communicates to students how they are encouraged to do their work. This sets up an environment that values understanding and academic growth and defines the intrinsic value of learning as a class goal.

Classrooms characterized as caring, supportive, inviting, and friendly are more likely to foster comfortable interaction with teachers and other students. Emphasizing mutual respect can contribute to a student's psychological safety and can reduce anxiety and the threat of making mistakes and contribute to a comfortable academic environment. This concept includes teaching and facilitating healthy interaction with student peers.

As a mentor, it is vital to help the new teacher become familiar with avoidance behavior and construct a clear message about the desired relationships students have with each other and the teacher. In this way they are likely to decrease the amount of help-avoidance behavior. Here are some points to examine with the new teacher:

- What are the spoken and unspoken norms and values in the classroom environment?
- Is it acceptable and encouraged for students to interact with their classmates on academic issues?
- Is learning expected to be done independently or collaboratively?
- What is acceptable behavior in response to the efforts of other students, their ideas, or questions?
- Being able to "read" the social climate within a class helps a teacher create a "hidden" curriculum designed to facilitate help-seeking behavior. New teachers may need help developing it.

Precautions and Possible Pitfalls

Some students have become traumatized by their school experiences over the years and are all but totally resistant to change. Older students can become so entrenched in avoidance behavior they have become untouchable or "teacher proof." The important message here is to give it the best shot but do no additional harm in the process. New teachers need to be careful that they don't make a bad situation worse by forcing themselves into a student's life. Unfortunately, experience in these matters is usually the best teacher once becoming aware of the issues. The teacher's ability to affect a situation will grow with time.

Source

Ryan, A. M., Pintrich, P. R., & Midgley, C. (2001). Avoiding seeking help in the classroom: Who and why? *Educational Psychology Review, 13*(2), 93–114.

STRATEGY 15: Help beginning teachers come to grips with the factors that influence motivation within their students and their classes.

What the Research Says

One hundred and sixty-three undergraduate education majors enrolled in an introductory educational psychology course became the subjects of research on the concepts of motivation in the classroom. These preservice teachers brought a wealth of knowledge about education to their education classes. While the researchers felt that their personal history–based prior knowledge served as an invaluable reference into which new knowledge about teaching and learning could be integrated, it also presented problems. Preservice teachers' conceptions of motivating their students to learn may not be compatible with the new theories and ideas presented in their education course work. Researchers found that most ideas about how best to motivate their students came from their own experiences or preconceived notions on the source of inspiration and motivation for learning.

This study found that research from student teaching has demonstrated that student teachers often see teaching as telling and learning as memorization. The researchers also cited a recent study that found that undergraduate education majors tend to think of effective motivators as being extrinsic (prizes, stickers, free time, candy) in nature rather than more intrinsic (choice, autonomy, challenge) in nature.

Further, a second study cited a number of other studies that pointed to the notion that intrinsically motivated students

- earn higher grades and achievement test scores, on average, than extrinsically motivated students;
- are better personally adjusted to school;
- employ "strategies that demand more effort and that enable them to process information more deeply";
- are more likely to feel confident about their ability to learn new material;
- use "more logical information-gathering and decision-making strategies" than do extrinsically motivated students;
- are more likely to engage in "tasks that are moderately challenging, whereas extrinsically oriented students gravitate toward tasks that are low in degree of difficulty";
- are more likely to persist with and complete assigned tasks;
- retain information and concepts longer and are less likely to need remedial courses and review; and
- are more likely to be lifelong learners, continuing to educate themselves outside the formal school setting long after external motivators such as grades and diplomas are removed.

Both articles point to the problem of a new teacher's lack of understanding regarding the factors involved in K–12 student motivation.

A greater understanding of motivational issues would empower the new teacher with a better understanding of the factors that maximize the motivational potential of the classroom-teaching-learning environment.

Application

It is clear that teachers pushing the right buttons can affect their students' level of motivation. School practices can and do affect a student's level of motivation. However, teachers tend to magnify their students' entry levels of motivation. They are drawn to the motivated students and tend to interact less with the motivationally low students. The motivated get "richer" or more motivated and the lower motivated students deteriorate further. New teachers can become frustrated with the low motivation of their students and may not have the background to recognize what they are feeling. Further, their teacher education programs may not have prepared them to consider the issue of motivation and motivation strategies. Here are a few suggestions that the research provided that mentors could share with new teachers in addition to their own ideas.

At the classroom level:

• Extrinsic rewards might work for a few, but the strategy soon becomes socially and environmentally divisive. Be careful and use extrinsic rewards sparingly. If extrinsic motivators are to be used, they are most effective when rewards are closely related to the task accomplished. Also, rewards should only be given when they are clearly deserved. Giving a prize for minimally successful work sends the message that minimum effort is acceptable, and the reward then becomes meaningless.

• Communicate classroom expectations for performance and behavior that are clear and consistent. Set clear standards that students understand as criteria (rubrics work well here) for individual assignments by giving them examples of high-, average-, and low-level work and be clear on how each piece was assessed and evaluated. Make sure the examples are within the intellectual bell curve of the class and remain reachable as standards.

• Make students feel welcome and supported and make the environment as much theirs as the teacher's. Students of all ages need to feel that teachers are involved in their lives. Take time to get to know students, talk to them individually, and express personal enjoyment in interactions with them.

• Respond positively to student questions and work.

• Try to create positive student-adult interactions, as the classroom may provide the only opportunity for this with some students, especially those at risk.

• Break down large tasks into more doable smaller goals. Doing so prevents students from becoming overwhelmed and discouraged by lengthy projects. Some students simply aren't capable of planning further than short periods at a time.

• Promote mastery learning. When a student completes an assignment that does not meet the expected criteria, give her or him one or more opportunities to tackle the task again, with clear direction on how to achieve the desired result. Be prepared to work directly with the student if necessary.

• Immediate feedback usually works best. Assess student work as soon as possible after completion and be sure that feedback is clear and constructive.

• Try to evaluate students individually if possible. Sometimes a weaker student's gains are proportionally greater than a stronger student's. Be sure to recognize them.

• Finally, develop ways to involve parents if possible. Discuss the issue of motivation with parents, involve them in efforts to increase their student's engagement, and suggest ways they can help.

In planning projects and activities and constructing curriculum, design pathways that are more interesting to students. Here are a few suggestions also suggested by the research:

• Build relevance into course materials by relating them to students' lives and highlight ways learning can be applied in real-life situations. Schoolwork should be meaningful to students in their real world, as well as within the classroom. Students are more engaged in activities when they can build on prior knowledge and draw clear connections between what they are learning and the world they live in.

• Allow students to have some degree of control over learning if possible. This can be done in any number of ways, from giving students choices between different assignments, to minimizing adult supervision over group projects, to letting students monitor and evaluate their own progress. The more responsible students feel for their own learning, the more ownership they will take.

• Create and assign challenging but achievable tasks and standards for all students, including at-risk, remedial, and learning disabled students. Stay away from busy work and try to keep the project open-ended enough to appeal to a wide range of learners. Students need to feel successful and that they've earned success.

• Arouse students' curiosity about the topic being studied. Controversy sells. Build it into lessons. Use the "mystery" approach, in which students are presented with fragmentary or contradictory information about a subject and are then asked to examine available evidence and their own feeling and thinking on the subject.

• Design projects that allow students to share new knowledge with others, including parents. More often than not, the teacher already knows all aspects of the curriculum and is not motivated to engage in a more "real life" conversation about the curricular knowledge. The teacher has no real need for the information the student would be providing. Learning is special and more engaging when students share what they are learning in reciprocal relationships. This is why group work works so well when done correctly.

Precautions and Possible Pitfalls

Learning the ins and outs of student motivation is almost best done by reflective experience. Timing is a factor that is difficult to explain. Why students turn on and off is often still a mystery to the most experienced teachers. Experience tells us that students, in spite of our best efforts, will sometimes disappoint us. Learning to accept the risks and disappointments of our efforts can be difficult when kids don't come through. New teachers can internalize this as failure on their part. Mentors can help new teachers deal with these feelings when their best efforts don't seem to work or the timing is simply wrong for the student.

Sources

Salisbury-Glennon, J. D., & Stevens, R. J. (1999). Addressing preservice teachers' conceptions of motivation. *Teaching and Teacher Education, 15,* 741–752.

Brewster, C., & Fager, J. (2000). *Increasing student engagement and motivation: From time-on-task to homework.* Northwestern Regional Education Laboratory. http://www.nwrel.org/request/oct00/textonly.html

3

Supporting New Teachers as They Organize Classroom Management and Discipline Policies

The art of teaching is the art of assisting discovery.

Mark Van Doren

 STRATEGY 16: *Introduce beginning teachers to student perspectives on effective class management.*

What the Research Says

Class management and discipline are what new teachers are most insecure about before entering the classroom. They are the essential prerequisites that allow other effective teaching and learning behaviors to be successful. Previous management research has largely focused on the teacher and the teacher's perspective. This research targets the assessment of the student perspective. The purpose of the study was to examine the students' view on teachers' behaviors that impeded or contributed to effective class management. Interviews with 182 students (100 males and 82 females) representing 14 different schools focused on teacher practices and student behavior. A wide selection of varying school contexts were utilized, but students provided consistent reports that effective managers set early, consistent standards and developed positive relationships with students.

Application

Certainly the focus on teacher perceptions of management is valuable, yet it would seem critical to also examine the students' perspective, as students are the impetus for teachers' decisions and actions. Teachers don't always want to know how their students are seeing their professional presence. It would be hard for most teachers to gather these data. This study seems to do it for them. In the introduction to this research, various other studies support the ideas that

- Students are cognizant of the appropriateness of different behaviors and can provide insights into why misbehavior occurs.
- Students hold clear conceptions of good teachers and what specific behaviors those teachers used in managing students.
- Students actively interpret and influence the learning environment and they may not attach the same meaning to various teacher behaviors. They don't assign the same meaning to the same classroom events as teachers or other observers.

So how do students see a successful classroom management program? Most students in the study felt that generally, classroom rules and behavior expectations were similar for most classes. If this is the case, what other factors make up an effective teaching strategy? What comes after making the rules?

Rules and standards are generally introduced at the beginning of a class and with students new to the teacher. After a "honeymoon period" students start to test the rules to find out what the "real" rules are and how the class is really going to function. Researchers found in this study that although testing of the standards and rules occurred, students expected and even wanted teachers who were consistent in administering a class management system. Many students complained about teachers who did not enforce class standards. When the rule testing did occur, students were adamant that teachers needed to have consistent and clear consequences in place. Students felt most teachers had similar consequences, but effective teachers actually used their consequences, while less effective teachers only threatened to use them. Ineffective cycles of threats and lack of follow through were cited as major concerns for students.

Students felt there were two reasons some teachers were not good managers:

- If they were strict, students would not like them, or
- Teachers didn't have the confidence to manage the class.

In addition to clear and consistent standards, students felt that effective class managers developed relationships with their students. Teachers who have respectful relationships with students are going to be trusted more. Students in this study saw themselves as equals and expected to be treated as such. Students wanted to be talked with and not at. Another way teachers lost respect was to lose control of their emotions. Students felt each such event was like the teacher giving up authority and respect.

Taking the time to seriously listen to students was deemed as important. Students in this study frequently named teachers as caring or uncaring, and these distinctions were critical in their discussions on class management. When teachers cared, the students also cared, and when teachers didn't care or appear to care, neither did the students.

Respect and caring relationships are not common topics in discussions of classroom management techniques. For some students, school is the only place where there is opportunity to have a sustained, quality relationship with a caring adult. Students reported that social and emotional distance in schools created more problems than they solved. Some felt it was important for teachers to initiate respect in the student-teacher relationship. Authority should be earned, not automatically given.

A mentor needs to realize that the interpersonal and communication skills described by students in this study were largely missing components of teacher education programs. In most schools the best teachers are described as exhibiting characteristics related to caring and respectful relationships with students. Students rarely cite content knowledge or pedagogy as important factors in accessing characteristics of good teaching. Ultimately it is a combination of professional personality, content knowledge, and instructional strategies that make up a teaching style.

Mentors can offer new teachers important insights regarding some of these more intangible characteristics of classroom management plans. Only more experienced teachers can put these qualities into words or explain how important they can be.

Precautions and Possible Pitfalls

 Inexperienced teachers may have a hard time implementing strategies regarding some of these ideas. The boundaries of a teacher's professional personality are created with experience. New teachers need to know that student relationships can be seen as works in progress, as students are also learning how to create and sustain working relationships. Some students will come through for teachers and others won't. Boundaries are always in flux, and teachers need to learn to read students for clues on where their comfort levels lie in classroom relationships. There is no one right formula.

Source

Cothran, D. J., Kulinna, P. H., & Garrahy, D. A. (2003). "This is kind of giving a secret away...": Students' perspectives on effective class management. *Teaching and Teacher Education, 19,* 435–444.

 STRATEGY 17: Encourage beginning teachers to learn about youth culture and use it to engage students in learning.

What the Research Says

It is no secret that some of the most difficult challenges facing beginning teachers are classroom management, physical and emotional isolation, and difficulty adapting to the needs and abilities of their students.

Brock and Grady (1997) concluded, "Teaching is one of the few careers in which the least experienced members face the greatest challenges and responsibilities" (p. 11). Many beginning teachers come prepared with book knowledge and theory but have little experience in controlling a classroom of 35 students. They tend to focus mostly on curriculum while wrongly assuming classroom control and discipline will just fall into place. The reality of how important maintaining classroom control is usually hits new teachers after the first few weeks of school when the honeymoon period is over for the students and they have figured out what they can and can't get away with in a particular class. This is one area where a mentor can provide critical assistance to help new teachers not only survive but thrive.

In many teacher preparation, induction, and mentoring programs across the nation, these issues are being addressed with concrete solutions and highly qualified mentors. Connecting with other exemplary veteran teachers who have experience and rapport with adolescents can also be a big help. New teachers at the secondary level report their teacher colleagues having a positive influence on helping them understand the challenges of adolescents. Conversely, elementary teachers felt their principals were extremely helpful in providing support and encouragement.

Application

No longer can we tolerate a "sink or swim" attitude. In California, the BTSA (Beginning Teacher Support and Assessment) program focuses on the beginning teacher learning as much as possible about the students in his or her classroom. Knowing which languages are spoken at home, previous student test scores, the community in which these students live, cultural and socioeconomic background, all help the new teacher understand and adapt to the needs of the students he or she teaches. Teachers need to keep up on the latest literature, music, language colloquialisms, clothing trends, and so on. They should spend time looking over popular magazines, checking on students' favorite films and television shows, and most importantly, taking time talking to and *listening* to kids.

Precautions and Possible Pitfalls

With the social climate today and students coming to class with a myriad of challenges and concerns, it is more important than ever for teachers to be aware of the problems and challenges of adolescent culture. What may seem trivial to an adult can be monumental to an adolescent. This is where the experience and training of a mentor can assist new teachers in understanding the culture and climate of students today. Most students would rather be considered "bad" in front of their peers than "stupid." However, many times a novice teacher will put a student in the position of acting out because he or she doesn't know the answer to a question. Perhaps there is a language barrier, or the student has been working late hours to help support his or her family and is unable to keep up with the workload at school.

It is also important that teachers not judge students based on what other teachers say. All students deserve a teacher who has not made up his or her mind on what the student is or is not capable of in the classroom. Another common mistake new teachers sometimes make (especially if they are close in age to their students) is that of becoming a buddy or friend—not retaining adult status, modeling adult ideas and behavior. The more a teacher can invest in understanding his or her students, where they are coming from, and what is important to them, the more successful the teacher can be in implementing classroom management procedures.

It is essential that the mentor accompany new teachers during their first few observations of exemplary teachers' classrooms. We ask new teachers to observe these outstanding colleagues, and yet many aren't sure just what they are supposed to be observing. Classroom management seems almost invisible, and transitions from one activity to another almost seamless. The new teacher may come away in awe that the veteran simply has the magic touch. A mentor can point out subtle nuances of effective classroom management and how a seemingly flawless transition is actually skillfully planned with procedures clearly in place.

Sources

Brock, B. L., & Grady, M. L. (1997). *From first-year to first-rate: Principals guiding beginning teachers.* Thousand Oaks, CA: Corwin.

Lortie, D. C. (1975). *Schoolteacher: A sociological study.* Chicago: University of Chicago Press.

STRATEGY 18: Remind beginning teachers to save their voices by engaging students in curricular conversations.

What the Research Says

Several recent studies suggest that teachers experience a higher frequency of voice-strain symptoms (67%) as compared with nonteachers (33%), regardless of their age (Smith, Gray, Dove, Kirchner, & Heras, 1997). On average a teacher talks for 6.3 hours during a typical school day (Siebert, 1999). In a study of more than 1,000 teachers, it was found that almost 21% had a pathological voice condition (Urrutikoetzea, Ispizua, & Matellanes, 1995).

Application

When observing a new teacher, take note of voice quality, volume, and pitch. New teachers may forget that the voice is a tool and can be used in a variety of ways depending on the circumstances. Consider video or audio taping a lesson to help open the conversation about the effective use of voice. New teachers frequently raise their voices as a way of compensating for noisy or disruptive students. When students are talking in competition with the teacher, the first thing a new teacher might do is raise his or her voice to either get students' attention or to drown out student raucousness. Add to this situation classrooms with loud ventilation systems, poor insulation between classrooms, and outside sources such as automobile traffic and aircraft overhead and it's no wonder teachers' voices become strained.

One of the most effective classroom management techniques in dealing with noisy or disruptive students is to actually reduce the volume of the teacher's voice to almost a whisper. This technique forces the student(s) to stop talking to be able to hear the teacher speaking. Often a teacher falls into the trap of raising his or her voice, sometimes to the point of yelling, a technique not generally considered effective in the long run. Many new teachers believe a louder voice will restore order. Discuss this tactic with the new teacher and how it may work in the short term, but soon students will just tune out. Suggest a far more effective method for the teacher to stop talking completely until the student or class is quiet.

Be prepared for the statement from the beginning teacher, "If I stop talking and teaching every time a student is talking out of turn, I'll never get the lesson taught." This is simply not the case. If a student or the class is talking or disruptive, they aren't listening to what the teacher is saying anyway. Teachers end up repeating instructions multiple times, losing valuable classroom time. Students will quickly learn that instruction stops when students aren't attentive. The key is for the teacher to resist the urge to shush students or to immediately return to talking once the noise begins to abate. Students need to learn early that instruction will stop and the focus of the lesson will not continue until everyone is quiet and paying attention. For the teacher this refrain from talking may seem like minutes, but, in actuality, it's usually only 15 to 20 seconds of wait time before the class is quiet.

Beginning teachers often think that if they aren't talking then they aren't teaching. Help the new teacher explore ways to give directions without using verbal instructions. Suggest writing directions on the chalkboard or put them on an overhead transparency. Another way to prevent voice strain is to establish procedures such as an agenda that is posted (to stop the 20 "what are we going to do today?" questions). Teachers should have procedures that don't require their voice in place for turning in homework, passing papers, asking a question, or getting into groups. With younger students, hand signals or a bell might signal it's time to get into groups.

Precautions and Possible Pitfalls

Feedback from mentors based on evidence (video tape of a lesson, audio tape of a lesson) may help new teachers see for themselves what effect their voices have in the classroom. When it comes to teaching, we need to remember the axiom "work smarter, not harder." Frequently new teachers forget that there are other ways of delivering the lesson besides direct instruction. With the short attention spans of students (of all ages), teachers need to explore alternative ways of instruction. A teacher's voice is an important instrument in teaching, and care should be taken to preserve it.

Sources

Siebert, M. (1999, February 7). Educators often struck by voice ailments. *The Des Moines Register*, p. 4.

Smith, E., Gray, S. D., Dove, H., Kirchner, L., & Heras, H. (1997). Frequency and effects of teachers' voice problems. *Journal of Voice, 11*(1), 81–87.

Urrutikoetzea, A., Ispizua, A., & Matellanes, F. (1995). Vocal pathology in teachers: A video-laryngostroboscopic study of 1,046 teachers. *Review of Laryngology, Otology, Rhinology, 116*(4), 255–262.

STRATEGY 19: Encourage beginning teachers to recruit a teaching partner as a peer coach.

What the Research Says

 In this study, the effects of peer coaching procedures were analyzed. In this case reciprocal peer coaching is described as teachers observing one another and exchanging support, companionship, feedback, and assistance in a coequal or nonthreatening fashion. Peer coaching is designed to foster a teacher's development and acclimation during periods of the development and introduction of new instructional practices in the classroom. This is in contrast to the traditional methods of staff development that rely on one-shot inservice training. Districts that inaugurate fundamental changes in the ways that teachers work, learn, and interact are also presumed to be more effective in addressing students' learning needs and capacities (Firestone & Bader, 1992; Little, 1990).

In this case, four teachers planned and conducted instructional innovation during the study on peer coaching relationships. They mixed and matched, completing the instructional planning and tasks both independently and with peer coaching. Outcomes measured the focus of teachers' collaboration with a peer coach, each teacher's procedural practices and refinements, a variety of student and teacher processes, and the teachers' ongoing concerns and satisfaction with the innovation. They found the following:

Three stages of different levels of need were identified as distinctive. Not surprisingly, they occur in a longitudinal fashion in Year 1 through Year 3. The first stage is described as survival, where teachers question their competence and desire to become teachers. Assistance takes the form of reassurance and specific skills almost on a daily basis as new teachers adapt to the transition into schools. In the second year, teachers have entered into a consolidation stage that focuses on instruction and the needs of individual students. In the third stage, renewal, teachers have become competent. Previously adopted activities and patterns have become routine and in some cases are not very challenging. In this stage teachers are looking for new ideas in their specialization.

Teachers working independently make few changes or refinements to their innovations. They made more changes and procedural refinements during peer coaching.

Many of the changes were sustained and reinforced in peer tutoring arrangements.

In a related study (Sparks & Bruder, 1987), it was found that 70% of the teachers who participated in coaching felt that their newly developed peer coaching technique produced marked improvement in students' academic skills and competencies.

Some educators have suggested that peer coaching and reciprocal learning help avoid isolation and foster communication, trust, and support. In this way it helps alleviate potential burnout.

Peer coaching provided promising solutions, enabling teachers to develop and tailor innovations to fit their personal teaching styles and needs at their site.

From a minority perspective, it was reported that some teachers felt it was a violation of traditional norms of autonomy, privacy, and equality in schools. Overall, the findings of the study support peer coaching strategies and suggest further refinement to help with some of the concerns voiced during the study.

Application

 Peer coaching works. New mentors or even an experienced mentor trying to improve his or her effectiveness will find it easy to transfer the results of this research to mentor-to-mentor relationships.

There is ample academic and professional literature on many versions of the technique. There are also many versions of these arrangements that can evolve into team mentoring or integrated or cooperative learning when new teachers from different content areas or backgrounds share the same mentor/peers and a similar curriculum or pedagogy.

Teachers and mentors involved in such relationships often feel much less isolated as teachers begin to know them well. Peer coaching shrinks the size of the school as teachers team together and share students and support each other's curriculum and instructional practices.

Many of these relationships begin informally; new teachers need to be open to these opportunities. Occasionally they are mandated. Participants need to know that effective collaboration can take practice and acclimation. New teachers may need to put their nervousness aside and go into this relationship feeling a little uncomfortable.

A little background research can also help new teachers find new ways to use peer coaching as they see how others utilize it in their settings.

Precautions and Possible Pitfalls

 Peer coaching can take time. Instead of doing grades or a million other things, the new teacher will need to be available to observe and plan with others. If this is a problem, consider peer relationships for a single unit or lesson and then move on. Teachers don't need to sustain peer coaching beyond its usefulness. Come together only when it is logical and practical.

Sources

Firestone, W. A., & Bader, B. D. (1992). *Redesigning teaching: Professionalism or bureaucracy?* Albany: State University of New York.

Kohler, F. W., Crilley, K. M., Shearer, D. D., & Good, G. (1997). Effects of peer coaching on teacher and student outcomes. *Journal of Educational Research, 90*(4), 240.

Little, J. W. (1990). Norms of collegiality and experimentation: Workplace conditions of school success. *American Education Research Journal, 19,* 325–340.

Sparks, G., & Bruder, S. (1987). Before and after peer coaching. *Educational Leadership, 3,* 54–57.

 STRATEGY 20: Ensure that beginning teachers actively address negative behaviors in their classrooms.

What the Research Says

 Based on her review of the current research, Garrick Duhaney (2003) lists effective practices for special educators. She advises that after using a functional analysis to produce a baseline, special education teachers should consider the following:

- Gradually introducing new routines and stimuli
- Focusing on transitions to prevent behaviors by warning students, using proximity control, redirecting inappropriate behaviors, and dismissing students in small groups rather than the whole group

- Evaluating the level of noise in a classroom, as many students are sensitive to noise and are distracted by the loudest ambient noise
- Addressing the personal connection by creating positive relationships (acknowledging birthdays, illness, knowing student names, etc.)
- Teaching interventions for behaviors including self-talk (moving from aloud to silent)
- Providing opportunities for physical movement
- Teaching the rules and avoiding no-win arguments
- Using token economies, contingency contracts, and cognitive behavioral therapy to teach more functional behaviors
- Using peer support, family involvement, and social skills interventions

She also recommended that teachers and parents visit the interactive website: www.behavioradvisor.com.

Application

Years ago, experts advised new parents to drop to their hands and knees to evaluate their home for potential hazards during their childproofing efforts. The same analogy can be applied to the classroom. By having beginning teachers view their classrooms through the eyes of their students, particularly those with behavioral issues, they will gain valuable insights into the best way to prevent negative behaviors.

During the coaching meeting, mentors can begin asking beginning teachers to evaluate the physical environment of their classrooms. Beginning teachers should consider the effects that the desk arrangement may have on the students who need to move around frequently. Mentors can discuss noise, temperature, as well as how the teacher uses the layout when teaching. Many mentors find that drawing a rough sketch of the classroom and drawing lines to indicate teacher movement and tally marks for students who are called on during an observation, provides concrete information that teachers may be unaware of until they see it in black and white. Mentors should note problem areas and either discuss how to adjust them or encourage the beginning teacher to teach students how to react appropriately to the situation if the environmental factor cannot be changed.

As part of the post-observation meeting, mentors should discuss classroom procedures. Although teaching specific classroom procedures rather than allowing students to discover the rules over time is time well spent, frequently beginning teachers feel they must rush right into the curriculum. Mentors should encourage beginning teachers to consider how they facilitate transitions, ensuring that they minimize abrupt changes and prepare students ahead of time for specific activities.

Beginning teachers may benefit from discussing the curriculum and its impact on the specific students in a class. Mentors can ask, "Are there concepts that seem to frustrate your students?" If the answer is affirmative, beginning teachers may need to prepare their students by letting them know that the material is challenging and reassure them that the material will be covered in several ways to facilitate their understanding.

Finally, beginning teachers may need to be reminded to consider the individual student. Having open communication with the student, parent, and other service providers will facilitate the student's efforts in improving behavior.

Precautions and Possible Pitfalls

Mentors should remind beginning teachers to give the changes they make in classroom environment, routine, or instruction time before evaluating their efficacy. After making a significant adjustment in their usual practice, it is normal to see a honeymoon period followed by an increase in negative behaviors prior to seeing the negative behavior diminish. Beginning teachers need to know that this is part of the process so they will refrain from making too many changes at one time.

Sources

Garrick Duhaney, L. M. (2003). A practical approach to managing the behaviors of students with ADD, *Intervention in School & Clinic, 38*(5), 267–280.

STRATEGY 21: Help beginning teachers fit everything in by making realistic time estimates during lesson planning.

What the Research Says

Teachers need to have excellent time-management skills for students to learn effectively. It is sometimes said that "time + energy = learning." Sometimes there's confusion between the time teachers allocate for instruction (e.g., a 50-minute class period) and the time students are actually engaged in learning, which may only be 25 minutes out of the 50 allocated. The concept of engaged time is often referred to as "time-on-task." Teachers often fail to take into account the off-task time they devote to managing student behavior, managing classroom activities, and dealing with announcements and interruptions.

Application

Often new teachers have difficulties realistically estimating the amount of time students will need to complete specific activities or assignments. Mentors should help new teachers distinguish between time allocated for instruction and engaged learning time when estimating how much time it will take for students to learn a particular set of material. During observations mentors should keep track of the time to share with new teachers so they have concrete data to compare with their estimates. Regular follow-up will help ensure improved accuracy in estimation skills. Mentors should remind new teachers that it's the time students actually spend learning that is the key to the amount of achievement.

Precautions and Possible Pitfalls

New teachers need to be sure to plan time in their lessons for students to digest the material covered, to monitor their comprehension of concepts and tasks, and to engage in clarification as needed. Mentors may want to share their own tips for handling the inevitable situation of an unplanned fire drill or an activity that ends too early. Looking at a lesson only from a teacher's point of view of making sure material is taught or covered, the new teacher is likely to underestimate the time students need to understand, record, and remember what they have learned. Teachers should make sure to allow sufficient note-taking time to help to ensure that students have time to take complete notes of the development being done in the lesson, so that they can effectively review for tests at home.

Source

Brophy, J. (1988). Research linking teacher behavior to student achievement: Potential implications for instruction of Chapter 1 students. *Educational Psychologist, 23,* 235–286.

4

Supporting New Teachers as They Develop Strategies for Managing Curriculum and Pedagogy

Genius is the ability to reduce the complicated to the simple.

C. W. Ceran

 STRATEGY 22: *Encourage beginning teachers to define themselves as teachers beyond their subject matter or content knowledge.*

What the Research Says

Knowing lots of information about or within a subject area will not ensure success as a teacher. This research (Kennedy, 1998) raises questions about what math and science teachers need to know to teach math and science well. The study begins by examining reform proposals for K–12 science and math teaching by defining what good teaching practices consist of. It does a literature search to delineate the varieties and types of knowledge that have been associated with this kind of teaching. The focus of the investigation is on subject matter knowledge but continues further to address the character of the knowledge rather than the content of the knowledge.

The types of knowledge identified by the research include conceptual understanding of the subject, pedagogical content knowledge, beliefs about the nature of work in science and math, attitudes toward the subjects, and actual teaching practices with students.

Unfortunately, the literature is incomplete with respect to which types of this knowledge base are relatively more or less important. Reform commentaries include many ideas about the character of knowledge, beliefs, and attitudes that teachers need to teach math and science in a new, less didactic way. Their comments characterize optimal teacher knowledge as:

- **Conceptual:** having a sense of size and proportion; understanding the central ideas in the discipline; understanding the relationships among ideas; and being able to reason, analyze, and solve problems in the discipline
- **Pedagogical:** having the ability to generate metaphors and other representations of these ideas based on the knowledge, ability, and experience level of the students
- **Epistemological:** having an understanding of the nature of work in the disciplines
- **Attitudinal:** having respect for, and an appreciation of, the processes by which knowledge is generated through the disciplines

There is one important reason, cited in the research, for teachers to possess a rich and deep understanding of their subject knowledge. Reformers want them to stop reciting facts to students and start encouraging students to explore the subject for themselves. Teachers confident in their knowledge can orchestrate this self-discovery with carefully designed teaching strategies and learning pathways.

To carry this idea of literacy further, the way teachers come to understand these proposed forms of discipline-based knowledge are appropriate outcomes not just for teachers but also for college-educated citizens. The limits of the study cite that these characteristics are not clearly understood in the context of actual teaching practices or the way that ideal practice is defined relative to actual practice.

Application

Many individuals new to teaching come with strong content or subject matter knowledge. Most have majored in a specific area in college or have years of knowledge gathered in the private sector as professionals. For new teachers, subject matter knowledge means a lot in defining themselves as teachers. Usually after a few years of teaching, teachers find that content knowledge plays a much smaller role in their success or failure as a teacher than they first thought. While content knowledge is important, it rarely defines the success or failure of a teacher. A teacher not only controls what students will know about a subject but how they come to know it and the context in which it exists.

The research looks into how content or discipline knowledge exists and is defined. It makes a clear distinction between what there is to know and how that material comes to be known. There is much more to know about subject matter content than just the facts. Evidence suggests that many teachers present their subjects as vast collections of facts, terms, and procedures with little connection among the components. They also present the facts as if they were self-evident and that students should accept and remember them without much thought. If teachers are to engage students in high-level thinking skills, teachers themselves must have a grasp of these ideas (the range of understanding knowledge) and must have a healthy respect for the difficulties of developing and justifying knowledge in their field.

Beyond the basics, a teacher should allow the students to use questions and misconceptions in guiding their exploration of subject matter and the nature of knowing. Be prepared to guide students to clarify confusion and to ensure that misconceptions are not perpetuated.

Be aware that some questions or hypotheses are beyond either the teacher's or the students' capacities to pursue or generate ideas and will lead the teacher and the lessons astray, down dead-end alleys, or into trivial pursuits. Teachers are not expected to move in any direction the class might want to go. Teachers learn to manage classroom direction by recognizing which questions or comments might be fruitful and which to stay away from.

Remember that covering just basic knowledge does not guarantee retention or usefulness. Very often it is *how* a person comes to know something that contributes to long-term retention and usefulness. Students must be motivated to guide the direction (curiosity and interest) in which knowledge is dispersed and acquired.

It also helps to keep in mind that knowledge in any discipline has a past, present, and future. Some learning has a finite shelf life and students need to understand that too.

The best thing a mentor can do is help a new teacher make the transition from content specialist to teaching specialist. Very few principals interview a prospective teacher on content knowledge, and the sooner new teachers begin to focus on learning to teach, the better.

Precautions and Possible Pitfalls

 A new teacher who is having trouble defining the boundaries of content knowledge should begin to consider a new term to add to educational jargon: *recitational* subject matter knowledge. It refers to the types of knowledge that have traditionally been tested in achievement tests in the past. Recitational knowledge also covers the ability to recite specific facts on demand, to recognize correct answers on multiple-choice tests, to define terms correctly, and to be good test takers. Many reformers think that traditional courses and curricula are limited to recitational knowledge. It is their aim to extend the character of discipline knowledge beyond this point.

Keep in mind that *what* to teach is usually more politically loaded than *how* to teach it or to know it. Also, covering material by incorporating superficial instructional techniques does little for retention. It only provides a false sense of security. Discipline knowledge must include having strategies that the teacher can use to provide context and relevance to recitational knowledge in order to cause true learning to occur.

Sources

American Association for the Advancement of Science. (1989). *Science for all Americans: A Project 2001 report on literacy goals in science, mathematics, and technology.* Washington, DC: Author.

Kennedy, M. (1998). Education reform and subject matter knowledge. *Journal of Research in Science Teaching, 35*(3), 249–263.

 STRATEGY 23: Help beginning teachers to establish scaffolds for complex skills and procedures.

What the Research Says

Walberg (1991) suggests that in science it is especially useful for students to struggle with interesting, meaningful problems that can stimulate discussion about competing approaches. This idea can be stretched to include all disciplines. He recommends using what he calls *comprehension teaching*, more commonly called *scaffolding*, which involves providing students with temporary support until they can perform tasks on their own. Based on Vygotsky's (1978) concept of the "zone of proximal development," scaffolding is recommended for teachers to build from what students can do only with temporary guidance from a more competent person, gradually reducing and eventually removing this support as students become independent thinkers and learners who can perform the task or use the skill on their own. The zone of proximal development refers to the area within which the student can receive support from another to successfully perform a task that he or she cannot perform independently. Scaffolding has been found to be an excellent method of developing students' higher-level thinking skills (Rosenshine & Meister, 1992). Scaffolding is a strategy for gradually and systematically shifting responsibility and control over learning and performance from the teacher to the student.

Application

Mentors should invite beginning teachers to assess students' abilities to perform and not perform important skills or tasks independently through a variety of methods (observation, listening, tests). Beginning teachers should test students' abilities to perform or not perform these skills or tasks with assistance from another, in order to conceptualize their zone of proximal development. Teachers can use a scaffolding approach for skills and tasks that are within the students' zone. Scaffolds can range from a simple hint, clue, example, or question to a complex sequence of activities that begin with teacher-centered approaches (explaining, demonstrating) but end as student-centered (self-questioning, self-monitoring).

Mentors may choose to share the following example, which is a scaffolding approach to teaching students to construct graphic organizers of text they have read. It is a complex sequence of steps that uses scaffolding to shift from teacher direction and control of creating graphic organizers to student self-direction and self-control over making them.

1. Show and explain a variety of traditional examples of graphic organizers, such as flow charts, concept maps, and matrices, made by both professionals and students.

2. Inform students about what graphic organizers are and when, why, and how to use various types of them. One source (Jones, Pierce, & Hunter, 1988/1989) provides information on why and how to create graphic organizers to comprehend text and it provides illustrations of a spider map, a continuum or scale, a series of events chain, a compare-contrast matrix, a problem-solution outline, a network tree, a fishbone map, a human interaction outline, and a cycle. Another source focuses on concept maps and Vee diagrams (Novak, 1998).

3. As classwork or a homework assignment, give students a partially completed graphic organizer to finish on their own. Give students feedback on their completions.

4. Assign classwork or homework that requires students to complete an empty graphic organizer structure entirely on their own. Give students feedback.

5. Assign classwork or homework requiring groups of students to create their own graphic organizers. Give students specific criteria or rubrics for constructing and evaluating graphic organizers. Sample criteria include (a) work is neat and easy to read, (b) ideas are expressed clearly, (c) ideas are expressed completely but succinctly, (d) content is organized clearly and logically, (e) labels or other strategies (colors, lines) are used to guide the reader's comprehension, (f) main ideas, not minor details, are emphasized, (g) work is visually appealing, and (h) the reader doesn't have to turn the page to read the words.

6. Once their graphic organizers are completed, the individual groups show their graphic organizers to the other groups, which critique the graphic organizers and give feedback based on the criteria identified above. Teachers should supplement the feedback as needed.

7. For homework, students develop graphic organizers completely on their own, using the identified criteria. Group members give each other homework feedback on the extent to which they met the established criteria.

8. Finally, students are expected to be able to create and critique their own graphic organizers, and support from others (students and teacher) isn't needed.

Precautions and Possible Pitfalls

Mentors should be aware that scaffolding is a complex task for many beginning teachers and mentors need to model appropriate scaffolding techniques to demonstrate their efficacy. To use scaffolding effectively it is vital for beginning teachers to consider issues such as what types of support to provide and when and what order to sequence them in, and to figure out the criteria for deciding when it is time to reduce or withdraw support from students. It is also very important to make sure scaffolding attempts are truly within the students' zone of proximal development. If they are below this area, activities will be too easy because the student can really do them independently. If they are above this area, no amount of scaffolding will enable students to perform independently because the skill or task is too difficult given the students' prior knowledge or skills.

Sources

Jones, B. F., Pierce, J., & Hunter, B. (1988/1989). Teaching students to construct graphic representations. *Educational Leadership, 46*(4), 20–25.

Novak, J. (1998). *Learning, creating and using knowledge: Concept maps as facilitative tools in schools and corporations.* Mahwah, NJ: Lawrence Erlbaum.

Rosenshine, B., & Meister, C. (1992). The use of scaffolds for teaching higher-level cognitive strategies. *Educational Leadership, 49*(7), 26–33

Vygotsky, L. S. (1978). *Mind in society: The development of higher psychological processes.* Cambridge, MA: Harvard University Press.

Walberg, H. (1991). Improving school science in advanced and developing countries. *Review of Educational Research, 61*(1), 25–69.

STRATEGY 24: *Support beginning teachers in expanding their use of rubrics as instructional tools.*

What the Research Says

Research has found that teachers at various academic levels are exploring the use of rubrics in their classes. In this general survey, teachers at all levels used rubrics for assessment and for many other purposes within their instructional practices. Each application transforms the rubric to another purpose, and the rubric can become a specialized instrument. Researchers investigating the use of rubrics in their own secondary methods courses found certain benefits and detriments in their use.

The benefits include reflective practice among students and instructors within the methods class and among the students using rubrics in their own classes. The detriments are related to issues of time and the clarity of the rubric's content. Researchers found that incorporating rubrics into instruction can benefit a course in two general areas. First, rubrics are tools that can be used to encourage reflective practice in both a temporal and a spatial sense. They model effective organizational strategies for students. Second, they are important in the development of professional knowledge through reflection and revisiting the rubric that is constructed. They force teachers to clarify the goals of the class and the goals of the specific lesson. Rubrics begin a discourse between students and teachers, and instruction, content, and assessment.

More specific detriments include a class "addiction" to rubrics in that they learn to depend on them. In addition, students and teachers find that once implemented, sometimes the rubric doesn't fit and needs modification; therefore, its validity suffers.

Researchers found that 75% of teachers who experienced rubrics in secondary science methods classes now used rubrics in their own classes. Overall, like concept maps and portfolios, rubrics, once mastered and practiced, prove to be a positive addition to the teacher's instructional toolbox.

Application

 The term *rubric* has been an educational buzzword for years. However, for a new teacher looking to create structure out of chaos and frantic thinking it may be just the right thing!

Before a discussion about rubrics can begin, it is important to clarify the term. The National Science Education Standards (National Research Council, 1996) states that a rubric is "a standard of performance for a defined population." Others have described rubrics as guidelines laid out for judging student work on performance-based tasks. They describe a rubric as an established set of criteria used for scoring or rating students' tests, portfolios, or performances. Consider the following questions when developing a rubric.

- What do we want students to know and be able to do?
- How much do we want students to know and be able to do?
- How will the teachers and other scorers know when the student knows it or does it well?

What new teachers need to know is there are no prescribed procedures for developing rubrics in education. Constructs are very dependent upon the context of their use or teacher expectations. A transfer of one rubric to another teacher and class simply would not work most of the time. Yet, examining rubrics from other classes is an important developmental activity and leads to professional growth.

One good suggestion for the construction of a rubric starts with writing performance standards. These can be found in many curriculum guides and frameworks. These standards should then be analyzed and divided into different components and complexity levels. The complexity and rigor of the rubric is then based on the experience and ability level of the students and a teacher's goals.

Development of rubrics can come from three perspectives: holistic, analytical, or a combination of both. Holistic rubrics are instruments that contain different levels of performance that describe both the quantity and the quality of the task. The instructor determines the best fit for aspects of the lesson for the students. Analytical rubrics are constructs that consist of criteria that are further subdivided into different levels of performance. Start with criteria to be assessed and move on to different levels of performance for the criteria. Analytical rubrics tend to be more precise and concise, while holistic rubrics contain broader descriptions about levels of performance.

Typing the word *rubric* into an Internet search engine can yield many good Web sites that can get a teacher started or can further refine and develop his or her rubric philosophy. Whichever style a teacher synthesizes as his or her own, the rubric should try to involve students in patterns of observation, reflection, thinking, and problem solving that reflect the standards of the community as reflected in various standards for content and processes.

Precautions and Possible Pitfalls

All teachers should keep in mind that a major long-term goal of instruction is to have students be able to decide, on their own, what they need to know, how they need to know it, and when they need to know it. Rubrics can create dependence and do not foster "learning how to learn" strategies unless a teacher deliberately builds this goal into his or her strategy to reduce the students' dependence on them.

At some point, teachers should try to have the students collaborate with him or her in the development of mutually agreed-upon rubrics. The exercise becomes guided practice in transferring some responsibility to the students for their own learning.

Source

Luft, J. A. (1999). Rubrics: Design and use in science teacher education. *Journal of Science Teacher Education, 10*(2), 107–121.

National Research Council (1996). *National education standards.* Washington, DC: National Academy Press. Retrieved July, 2002 from bob.nap.edu/readingroom/books/nses/html/5.html#dsdl

Strategy 25: Encourage beginning teachers to develop the art of questioning by building in wait time.

What the Research Says

There is an art to questioning that is frequently overlooked by novice teachers. While teachers spend time planning lessons, designing assessment, and grading homework, little thought is given to the importance of using questioning in a student-centered classroom. Of particular importance, but often neglected, is the concept of "wait time."

Wait time may be defined as the time a teacher waits after asking a question before talking again (Rowe, 1986). Too often a teacher asks a question and then expects an immediate response. Research shows that the longer the pause (three to five seconds), the more thoughtful the response.

Wait time is especially useful when asking higher-order questions. A study of preservice teachers who observed middle and high school science classes on the East Coast reported that with little or no wait time, short answers were elicited. When the wait time was increased, the caliber of answers was greater (Freedman, 2000). In this same study, teachers reported that on a typical day they asked about 24 questions in a 40-minute class period. The number of convergent questions was twice that of divergent ones, and they asked the same percentage of lower-order questions (knowledge and comprehension) as higher-order questions (application, analysis, synthesis, and evaluation). When asked what they could do to expand into more desirable questioners, their answer was "more planning."

Application

Beginning teachers need to plan and practice the types of questions they will be asking their students. Questioning can be used for many purposes, including checking for understanding, determining students' prior knowledge, beginning a class discussion, or stimulating critical thinking. Questions should be part of the lesson planning process and should be planned just as other parts of the lesson are. The simple counting to self (one-thousand one, one-thousand two, . . .) can help remind new teachers to wait after asking a question.

Mentors can help new teachers evaluate and improve their questioning practices. Having the observer write down the questions asked, while the lesson is being taught, and then reflecting back on that lesson can be useful in assisting the new teacher in the improvement of his or her practice. Another excellent method for reflection is to videotape the teacher teaching a lesson. The new teacher can then see how questions were asked, if they were convergent or divergent, and the amount of wait time allowed. All of these factors can help the novice learn his or her craft.

Precautions and Possible Pitfalls

Mentors should remind new teachers not to get caught up in always asking the same type of questions, asking the same students, and expecting a correct answer each time. When asking a question of a specific student, it is important that other students do not shout out the answer if the designated student doesn't answer immediately. Sometimes it is better to ask the question first, then call on a student. This will help reduce student passivity. In addition, if the teacher asks questions that invite reflection, the learning comes about as a result of a partnership between teacher and student.

Sources

Freedman, R. L. H. (2000). [Questioning strategies in Western New York teachers' science classrooms]. Unpublished raw data.

Rowe, N. B. (1986). Wait-time: Slowing down may be a way of speeding up. *Journal of Teacher Education, 37*(1), 43–50.

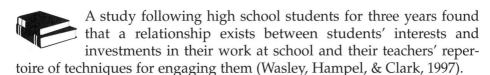

Strategy 26: Help beginning teachers to develop a variety of instructional strategies to stimulate student interest.

What the Research Says

A study following high school students for three years found that a relationship exists between students' interests and investments in their work at school and their teachers' repertoire of techniques for engaging them (Wasley, Hampel, & Clark, 1997).

Application

Mentors may want to engage their beginning teachers in a brainstorm about high interest instructional strategies. Although establishing routines is an important part of the beginning teacher's practice, too much predictability can cause students' interest to wane.

Using a range of instructional strategies from one unit to the next stimulates student interest. For example, a teacher might have students listen to a speech, discuss it in a group, and then write a paper about the speech. Following this project the teacher may have students do a group assignment about favorite speeches and the people who gave them. Students could finish up this unit by either delivering their favorite speech or writing one of their own. A steady diet of reading the book, answering the questions at the end of the chapter, listening to a lecture or watching a video, and taking a test does not provide for good instruction.

Essential to the success of varying instructional strategies is support from school districts in providing professional growth opportunities for teachers by encouraging them to attend workshops or seminars or to network with colleagues about best teaching practices. Mentors should make the effort to locate these kinds of opportunities for their beginning teachers.

One of the most critically important aspects of the mentor process is the reflection with the teacher after a lesson is taught. Reflection provides opportunities to examine specific instructional strategies and their effectiveness with a specific class or student population. Another powerful strategy is to invite observation by colleagues or other mentors. An observation of a novice teacher's lesson and the reflective conversation afterward can be a "mirror" to the novice of what is really going on in the classroom. These mentors can help novice teachers understand that mirroring is essential to their development as professionals.

In many teacher induction programs around the country, districts are now focusing on helping new teachers build a repertoire of techniques, skills, and strategies through ongoing professional development. Districts must allow time for new teachers to attend seminars, conferences, and observations of exemplary teachers to assist these emerging teachers in building a repertoire that is responsive to the students they serve.

Precautions and Possible Pitfalls

Beginning teachers often fall into a pattern of using a particular strategy (especially if it has been successful) to the detriment of using any others. Although it is important for new teachers to take risks in the classroom, it is just as important to learn what works and what doesn't in a particular classroom setting. Students like consistency and routine to a point; however, if the instructional strategies are never varied, the students become bored and uninterested. It is important for mentors to remind beginning teachers that no one technique or strategy works every time with every student.

Source

Wasley, P., Hampel, R., & Clark, R. (1997). *Kids and school reform.* San Francisco: Jossey-Bass.

 STRATEGY 27: *Assist beginning teachers in using student peers to scaffold student learning.*

What the Research Says

 Peer tutoring can promote learning at virtually all grade and school levels. Research shows that peers can scaffold each other's development of higher-level thinking and learning. One study of seventh graders learning science assigned students to three tutoring conditions: explanation only, inquiry with explanation, and sequenced inquiry with explanation. Students were assigned to tutoring pairs and trained to tutor.

Tutoring occurred over five weeks on content the teacher had already covered. Researchers measured cognitive, metacognitive, and affective variables. The results showed that students do not have to be with other students who are more competent to develop their own thinking and knowledge. Students who are the same age and ability levels helped each other learn in all three conditions (King, Staffieri, & Adelgais, 1998).

A whole classroom of students helping other students has been found to be an efficient and effective method of enhancing achievement. Twenty teachers participated in a study of classwide peer tutoring with 40 classrooms in elementary and middle schools. Half of the schools implemented classwide peer tutoring programs and half did not. Both urban and suburban schools participated in the study, and students came from diverse backgrounds, both culturally and linguistically. There were three categories of students: average achievers, low achievers without learning disabilities, and low achievers with learning disabilities.

The peer tutoring programs were conducted 3 days a week, 35 minutes a day, for 15 weeks. Stronger students were paired with weaker students. Teachers reviewed each pair to ensure they were socially compatible. In all pairs, students took turns serving in the roles of tutor and tutee. Student pairs worked together for four weeks; then teachers arranged new pairings. Teachers received training on how to train their students to be tutors. Tutor training included teaching students how to correct each other's errors.

Achievement tests were administered before and after the peer-tutoring program. Regardless of whether students were average achievers or low achievers, with or without learning disabilities, students in the peer tutoring classrooms achieved at higher levels than those in the classrooms without classwide peer tutoring.

Application

Mentors know there are many areas in all disciplines that lend themselves to a peer tutoring program. When there is a skill or skills to be learned and all one needs is experience with success or in understanding something covered by the teacher or text, then peer tutoring can provide an efficient way to monitor and support a student trying to master the skill or knowledge.

Disciplines other than math may have a full range of student math competencies within the same class. If a student has difficulty with a math problem within an activity in a discipline other than math, and the student hasn't had geometry, others in the class might have and can act as tutors. Part of the student's problem is to recognize which calculation is called for and when more than one type of calculation may be used. It can get doubly confusing. Here a peer tutor (under the guidance of a teacher) can be quite beneficial. A student who has difficulty doing dilution factors or converting moles could find a peer tutor a genuine asset in a chemistry class. Additionally, the tutor, in explaining the calculation to the student, is also provided with an opportunity to strengthen his or her own understanding of both the concept of the application (a higher-order thinking skill) and the role of math in science. Thus, there is often a mutual benefit to a peer tutoring program.

Precautions and Possible Pitfalls

Mentors should ensure that a tutor-training program is offered by the teacher and must precede peer tutoring. Tutors must be given some instruction on how to conduct the sessions, what sort of difficulties to look for on the part of the tutee, and what points to stress in the sessions (based on the teacher's assessment of the class). Any individual difficulties on the part of the tutees should be mentioned to the tutor prior to the sessions. Tutors should be taught to guide student learning and not merely solve problems for students. Students with severe learning disabilities may pose a challenge to classwide peer tutoring, unless the tutors first receive individualized instruction from learning disabilities specialists.

Sources

Fuchs, D., Fuchs, L., Mathes, P. G., & Simmons, D. (1997). Peer-assisted learning strategies: Making classrooms more responsive to diversity. *American Educational Research Journal, 34*(1), 174–206.

King, A., Staffieri, A., & Adelgais, A. (1998). Mutual peer tutoring: Effects of structuring tutorial interaction to scaffold peer learning. *Journal of Educational Psychology, 90*(1), 134–152.

 STRATEGY 28: Encourage beginning teachers to make the most of one-on-one student contacts.

What the Research Says

 Frequent contact between teachers and students helps students develop academically and intellectually. Rich teacher-student interaction creates a stimulating environment, encourages students to explore ideas and approaches, and allows teachers to guide or mentor individual students according to individual needs.

Application

Beginning teachers will find that working with individual students in a traditional classroom setting is not practical for long periods of time. Mentors should advise that while students are working individually on an exercise, the teacher should visit with individual students and offer them some meaningful suggestions. Such suggestions might include hints on moving a student who appears frustrated or bogged down on a point toward a solution.

These private comments to students might also be in the form of advice regarding the form of the student's work. That is, some students are their own worst enemy when they are doing a geometry problem and working with a diagram that is either so small that they cannot do anything worthwhile with it or so inaccurately drawn that it, too, proves to be relatively useless. Such small support offerings will move students along and give them that very important feeling of teacher interest.

Mentors should point out that in some cases, when a student experiences more severe problems, the teacher might be wise to work with individual students after class hours. In the latter situation, it would be advisable to have the student describe the work as it is being done, trying to justify his or her procedure and explain concepts. During such one-on-one tutoring sessions, the teacher can get a good insight into the student's problems. Mentors may advise teachers to question, are the problems conceptual? Has the student missed understanding an algorithm? Does the student have perceptual difficulties or spatial difficulties? And so on.

Precautions and Possible Pitfalls

Mentors should caution new teachers that working with individual students and merely making perfunctory comments, when more might be expected, could be useless when considering that the severity of a possible problem might warrant more attention. New teachers should make every effort to give proper attention to students when attempting to react to this teaching strategy. Teachers should keep the student's level in mind so that, where appropriate, they can add some spice to the individual sessions by providing a carefully selected range and choice of challenges to the student so that there may be a further individualization in the learning process. Teachers should make sure good students don't get bored. Challenge them by giving them more difficult problems to solve, having them tutor other students, or having them evaluate alternative approaches to solving a problem.

Mentors should advise new teachers that some students can become very needy. They often lack confidence or the ability to work comfortably in an independent manner. This can compel them to begin to dominate class time. When this occurs, new teachers should give them the same general attention that they give to others. When their demands begin to dominate the class, new teachers can invite them to stay after school or at a time when they can receive undivided attention. Mentors may share that to conserve time, beginning teachers could consider combining a few students with the same problems and addressing their needs together. Or have students who understand the material serve as tutors, mentors, or group leaders.

Source

Pressley, M., & McCormick, C. (1995). *Advanced educational psychology.* New York: HarperCollins.

 STRATEGY 29: Encourage beginning teachers to increase their understanding of student learning styles.

What the Research Says

Tobias (1986) characterized introductory college science courses by negative features such as failure to motivate student interest, passive learning, emphasis on competitive rather than cooperative learning, and reliance on algorithms rather than understanding. These features sometimes steer students away from careers in the sciences. Recent research suggests that the mismatch between teaching practices and students' learning styles may account for many of these problems. Felder's (1993) model of learning styles is especially appealing because it conceptualizes the dimensions of sensing-intuiting, visual-verbal, inductive-deductive, active-reflective, and global-sequential as continuums rather than as dichotomous either/or variables. Felder cites research to guide instruction for each of these styles.

Application

Felder recommends the systematic use of a few additional teaching methods that overlap learning styles and contribute to the needs of all students. Mentors should encourage beginning teachers to use a variety of instructional approaches. These include giving students experience with problems before giving them the tools to solve them; balancing concrete with conceptual information; liberally using graphic representations, physical analogies, and demonstrations; and showing students how concepts are connected within and between subjects and to everyday life experience.

Precautions and Possible Pitfalls

Students and parents often have an entrenched view of how a specific class is presented and will be experienced. If a beginning teacher ventures too far from the norm, the students' comfort level can drop and their anxiety rises. If the beginning teacher feels that he or she is presenting teaching or learning experiences (restructuring or reforming) that might be new or unfamiliar, the teacher should consider clearly communicating these new strategies early. New teachers do not want to threaten students' potential success in their class or produce unneeded frustration.

Mentors need to beware of the dangerous tendency for new teachers to fall into the trap of labeling students, or allowing them to label themselves, as particular types of learners and restricting teaching and learning to the dominant styles. Ignoring nondominant styles can limit students' intellectual growth and development. The goal of thinking about students' learning styles is to facilitate learning—not constrain it.

Beginning teachers shouldn't expect miracles of themselves. There can be an overwhelming number and variety of learning styles within a particular class, and it's unrealistic for teachers to regularly accommodate instruction to all of them. The key is to vary instructional methods and present information in multiple modalities.

Sources

Felder, R. (1993, March/April). Reaching the second tier: Learning and teaching styles in college science education. *Journal of College Science Teaching, 23,* 286–290.

Tobias, S. (1986, March-April). Peer perspectives on the teaching of science. *Change,* 36–41.

STRATEGY 30: Remind beginning teachers that less equals more when they are streamlining the content of their curriculum.

What the Research Says

Eylon and Linn (1988) report that, cognitively, students respond better to a systematic, in-depth treatment of a few topics than they do to a conventional in-breadth treatment of many topics. Increasingly it is recommended that teachers, of all subjects, streamline the curriculum and focus more on a limited set of knowledge and skills. Students' misconceptions and lack of understanding of basics reflect limitations of mental processing and memory. Ted Sizer, a well-known progressive educator, identifies "less is more" as one of the major principles to guide educational reform. For more information, see "Less Is More: The Secret of Being Essential" in *Horace*, the online journal of the Coalition of Essential Schools Web site at www.essentialschools.org.

Application

 New teachers should examine the course(s) preceding theirs that students must take to get the background for their course and examine the courses following theirs for which students are expected to acquire the background. They can also compare the book content with the district's curricular guidelines or other types of content standards. Teachers may then use this information to identify the key information their course must cover. Once these decisions have been made, a teacher can then eliminate chapters of the textbook from the course to prevent overload and rote learning.

Most new teachers are overly worried about "coverage" at the expense of good teaching. Most experienced teachers know that coverage strategies give you only a false sense of security about what the students remember or are able to do with the new information. Quick coverage without true engagement in the curriculum is a waste of the teacher's and students' time.

Precautions and Possible Pitfalls

Don't throw out "diamonds in the rough," potentially interesting learning pathways, or favorite topics. There's a lot to be said for the effects of teacher enthusiasm for specific concepts, topics, and content on student motivation. A wise teacher will use them. The teacher just may have less time to spend on them.

Sources

Cushman, K. (1994, November). Less is more: The secret of being essential. *Horace,* 11(2), 1–4.

Eylon, B., & Linn, M. (1998). Learning and instruction: An examination of four research perspectives in science education. *Review of Educational Research, 58,* 251–301.

STRATEGY 31: *Encourage beginning teachers to use the opportunities provided by out-of-school learning environments.*

What the Research Says

 Learning outside of school (informal education) plays a vital role in the development of competence in language, reading, mathematics, and a variety of other school-related domains. Assume that such learning also contributes to classroom learning, motivation, and attitudes. Informal learning experiences help preschool children acquire a wide range of early literacy before the children enter school. They learn a language, usually before entering any formal classroom.

In this study, structured interviews of parents of elementary school children revealed the nature and scope of children's science-related activities outside of school. Research exposed a remarkable level of participation in extracurricular, science-related activities. Categories of participation included both nonfiction and science fiction television shows as well as reading activities, computer use, community activities such as zoos, home observations and simple science experiments, questioning and discussion, and household interest and familiarity with science. Often, time and interaction with science-related activities outside the formal science classroom exceeds time in the classroom.

While this study of informal learning looked primarily at science activities, it would come as no surprise to find the same sort of informal connections to other disciplines.

Application

The studies make it clear that learning outside of school should not be ignored and can be a new source of motivating instructional strategies. For example, if science students are required to spend only a few hours a week in science instruction, the overall role schooling plays in developing science literacy is questionable. Many theme parks and other organizations offer less threatening science experiences. Looking at real art in galleries and museums is often very different from most secondary art classrooms. The influence of home and community environments needs to become a factor in planning more formalized content instruction. Teachers are often surprised at the number of places that students visit with their parents. These places are rich sources of motivation and interest and include zoos, all types of museums, art galleries, and even amusement parks with "edutainment" components. If these places are interesting to students and can connect them to curricular agendas, learn to use them.

If new teachers are new to the community, turn them on to the potential the local community holds for enriching the curriculum with local flavor. Simple structured interviews or questionnaires can yield insights and characterize the development of content thinking from outside the school boundaries. This knowledge can yield a perspective on common experiences (e.g., exhibits at a museum) that can facilitate discussions, interpret phenomena, and frame classroom lessons and activities. Information could also serve to highlight a range of motivations and competencies among students and help teachers identify areas in which student "experts" could make a contribution to classroom learning, content projects, or other activities. It also can help identify influential allies at home who can reinforce a teacher's efforts with individual students or act as a broader class resource.

There is a full range of informal content-related activities students bring to a class. While this informal activity or exploration may diminish or change as students get older, much of their background and attitudes are based on this informal education. It may also become more specialized as a student finds some disciplines more interesting than others.

By remaining cognizant of the influence home and community environments have on overall content literacy, new teachers can begin to incorporate the information into their instructional practices. Creative teachers can explore, enhance, and develop a range of curricular connections to the students' informal background.

Precautions and Possible Pitfalls

School learning is often seen in a less enjoyable and sometimes more threatening light than the informal learning students encounter outside of the classroom. Much of the students' experience outside the classroom can be classified as edutainment. Integrating the two realms is a challenging but very doable task. Research into the connections is just beginning to illuminate instructional relationships and doesn't yet offer a wide range of tested curricula to use the knowledge. Don't let the lack of formal connections be discouraging. Mentors should help new teachers develop their own strategies to integrate the two paradigms within their instruction objectives and comfort zones.

Using resources outside the classroom can be a source of inequity due to access problems. Not all students have supportive parents or parents who can provide resources. If students are to be asked to visit or use resources outside of the classroom, offer a classroom or school-based option to those who can't participate off-campus.

Sources

Korpan, C. A., Bisanz, G. L., Bisanz, J., Boehme, C., & Lynch, M. A. (1997). What did you learn outside of school today? Using structured interviews to document home and community activities related to science and technology. *Science Education, 81*(6), 651–662.

5

Supporting New Teachers as They Develop, Use, and Evaluate Student Assessment Instruments

Education's purpose is to replace an empty mind with an open one.

Malcolm Forbes

An education isn't how much you've committed to memory, or even how much you know. It's being able to differentiate between what you do know and what you don't.

Anatole France

STRATEGY 32: *Encourage beginning teachers to consider alternate assessment styles and instruments for selected activities.*

What the Research Says

This research began by looking at Frank Oppenheimer, the originator of the Exploratorium in San Francisco, who argued against formal assessment in science centers and moved on from there. He saw the inherent value of informal learning in promoting science education and science and opposed the dominant, narrow view of science education taken in traditional, in-school science.

Because informal learning is not graded, no one flunks an informal encounter with science. This view can be shared within other disciplines.

Some researchers believe that many informal experiences are so individual and multifaceted that they cannot be assessed with letter grades or scores. Some progressive teachers see the lack of evaluation as an obvious strength. Engaging a student in subject content in a more social, open-ended, learner-directed center or environment is much less threatening and may enhance actual learning. Trying to evaluate so many potential unintended outcomes is just not fair to students. Out of four research papers that examined out-of-school informal educational activities, all used students' written reflections (some used a rubric to guide students' responses) to survey the students' perceptions of how much they learned and the quality of that learning.

Application

Once teachers and their students leave the classroom environment, lesson planning and assessment and evaluation can get messy. Goals and objectives become harder to define. In the case of out-of-school encounters cited, assessment instruments identified in this research were not designed to yield a score or grade. They were designed to measure the overall effectiveness of the encounter.

This information could then be used to modify the encounter itself and not rate the students' success or failure. Movies, plays, art galleries, and a host of other out-of-classroom activities can be used as authentic curricula that can provide interesting and motivating learning pathways.

One study featured assessment that was produced by parents interacting with their children. Students were stimulated by their parents' involvement and the students felt comfortable with their parents. Researchers found this type of assessment to suffer from low reliability and validity, but it had its advantages. The collaborative, nonthreatening nature of the informal project fostered active and meaningful learning and an integrated school, home, and community. It's clear that traditional content assessment may miss the point of the out-of-school experience or informal in-school learning.

There is a wider range of attributes and facets that need to be measured, and a content test would send the wrong message to students about what is important. Extending the experience by expanding it with a related performance-based project, writing activity, or other application would be a better gauge of mastery than a traditional test. The author of the research felt that projects with appropriate scoring rubrics, where students combine discipline content from the classroom and the informal experience, are the best way for students to demonstrate this type of learning. Ultimately all teachers want to facilitate growth of enthusiasm and motivation.

Teachers without experience working these types of experiences into their instructional strategies could benefit from some mentoring. Some schools have a pattern of utilizing community resources. Sharing what others in the school have done is a beginning. In addition, it would be useful to explore the off-site resources that local students might have utilized or informal opportunities that offer potential educational experiences. Once that's done, evaluation and assessment can be worked out.

Precautions and Possible Pitfalls

Consider a student who performs poorly in the traditional classroom yet exhibits enthusiasm and interest in more hands-on activities and participation in out-of-school learning experiences. This situation presents teachers with a dilemma as to how to encourage students like this and not penalize them with narrow-range, traditional classroom assessment devices.

The teacher should not turn the students' enthusiasm off. Balancing opportunities for successful assessment and evaluation gives students in this group more than one pathway to find and demonstrate success. Oral presentations, project display boards, student videos, computer-generated presentations (e.g., PowerPoint), and other instructional outcomes can help these students find success.

Another problem is providing equal access and opportunity for all students in class. Sometimes parental support is not available to all students. The teacher needs to make learning outside the classroom an option with an in-school component for those who can't participate in off-campus activities. In a marine biology class in a high school located near the coast, an intertidal visit and beach walk had an alternative in-class option for those who couldn't get to the beach during low tides.

Sources

Korpan, C. A., Bisanz, G. L., Bisanz, J., Boehme, C., & Lynch, M. A. (1997). What did you learn outside of school today? Using structured interviews to document home and community activities related to science and technology. *Science Education, 81*(6), 651–662.

Kurth, L. A., & Richmond, G. (1999). Moving from outside to inside: High school students' use of apprenticeship as a vehicle for entering the culture and practice of science. *Journal of Research in Science Teaching, 36*(6), 677–697.

Ramsey-Gassert, L. (1997). Learning science beyond the classroom. *Elementary School Journal, 97*(4), 433–450.

 STRATEGY 33: Emphasize the need for beginning teachers to give their students explicit, detailed feedback rather than just marking student responses right or wrong.

What the Research Says

Feedback is important for students in several ways: It helps them assess their mastery of course material, helps them assess their use of thinking and learning strategies, and helps them connect their efforts and strategies to their academic outcomes. The primary benefit of feedback is the identification of errors of knowledge and understanding and the assistance with correcting those errors. Feedback generally improves subsequent performance on similar items. Research suggests feedback can guide students in their use of learning strategies and that adults who try different strategies and are tested on their learning can generally identify effective strategies (Crooks, 1988).

Application

Mentors can share their experience that going beyond simply marking items right or wrong and giving students a score on a test allows students to have better ideas about how they went wrong. Making comments stimulates students' thinking about their errors. If grading time is a factor, beginning teachers should consider oral test reviews. They should find ways to reward students for authentically engaging in correcting student misconceptions and wrong answers. Mentors should remember that some disciplines are easier than others to do this with. New teachers should consider offering a pretest over the same concepts they will cover on the actual test. Rewarding the students who take the time to correct their mistakes on the pretest gives the new teacher another teachable moment with the class or individuals. The more motivated students will take advantage of the opportunity.

Precautions and Potential Pitfalls

 Mentors know that teachers spend many hours grading papers, writing comments, and giving feedback. However, there is always doubt as to how much students read and internalize the comments after seeing the score. Many students are not concerned with really knowing the test's content and scientific concepts. Mentors may suggest as an alternative that new teachers try to structure class time during activities or quiet assignments to give verbal rather than written feedback. They will receive feedback and get to know their students better.

Source

Crooks, T. (1988). Impact of classroom evaluation practices on students. *Review of Educational Research, 58*(4), 438–481.

 STRATEGY 34: *Teach beginning teachers how to use assessment strategies to inform instructional goals for powerful learning.*

What the Research Says

 In a critique of 309 lesson plans from 65 student teachers attending a large Midwestern state university, it was found that none contained all of the criteria that were deemed necessary for evaluating learning. The problems identified included

- An absence of a direct link between instructional goals and assessment
- Twenty-three percent that featured no observable objectives, although the majority recognized the need
- Samples of 103 assessments where only 8 assessment strategies were deemed complete
- The absence of reliability and validity concepts
- A huge discrepancy between measurement instruction from their university classes and its practical application among student teachers

Application

For new teachers in public education, there has never been a better time in which to find help on assessment and instructional practices. But they may need some help finding the resources. Today's course content has never been more analyzed by state framework writers, educational agencies, special interest groups, and parent organizations. The best of these analyses feature not only content outlines but pedagogical and assessment suggestions and guidelines. In addition, most textbook publishers (who design their books based on the same documents) provide instruction and assessment strategies connected to their book's content.

Most subjects' content frameworks are now accessible via the Internet, and a master or supervising teacher can access his or her content textbook's support material. In addition, many veteran teachers use assessment strategies that connect to skills required on standardized tests. The new teacher should analyze and use them all within his or her personal instructional context. It's clear that the resources are there. The dilemma for new teachers is deciding which to use. Some of these resources offer more valid and reliable information, and the trick is finding a secure bridge between instructional goals, classroom instruction, and assessment. Also, all new teachers have their own ideas about assessment or they adopt their master teachers' goals. Some framework and supplemental textbook information seems written by people who have never been in a classroom. Some others will stand out and seem to have been written just for the new teacher with his or her goals in mind. Beginning teachers should survey as much information as they can access before synthesizing their own strategies.

The trick for new teachers is to construct the unit or lesson in a complete package with equal attention to goals and objectives; instructional delivery systems; and fair, reliable, and valid assessment strategies. If assessment is considered and addressed before beginning instruction, the teacher will find peace of mind and security as he or she moves the students toward final assessment. The teacher will know what his or her students need to be successful as the lesson progresses and will always have that in the back of his or her mind. In this way the teacher can always make adjustments to instruction and shorten or lengthen the pace, simplify or rework instructional trouble spots, or tweak the assessment a bit if necessary. There is a saying that if you don't know where you are going, you will probably never get there. With assessment, teachers should take it to heart; their students will thank them and they will feel much more confident as teachers.

Precautions and Possible Pitfalls

For a new teacher, politics plays a heavy role in assessment. New teachers often find themselves split between using their master teachers' assessment instruments and strategies and developing their own. A solution to this dilemma is to co-develop the lesson or unit, including assessment, with the supervising mentor. Teachers should develop a resource bank of frameworks and other guidelines of their own and bring them to the table with them to support their ideas and their practices.

Also, students are often quick to blame the teacher for their lack of success on the assessment. The teacher needs to be prepared for these arguments. This is where veteran teachers can offer suggestions and help the beginning teacher as he or she prepares strategies for such situations, as they are better able to provide strategies due to their experience.

Source

Campbell, C., & Evans, J. A. (2000). Investigation of preservice teachers' classroom assessment practices during student teaching. *Journal of Educational Research, 93*(6), 350.

 STRATEGY 35: Familiarize beginning teachers with state and national standards to establish benchmarks for assessing student literacy.

What the Research Says

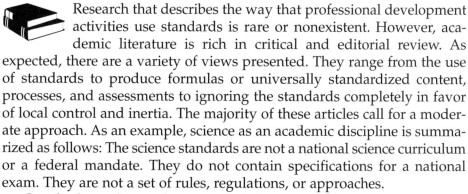 Research that describes the way that professional development activities use standards is rare or nonexistent. However, academic literature is rich in critical and editorial review. As expected, there are a variety of views presented. They range from the use of standards to produce formulas or universally standardized content, processes, and assessments to ignoring the standards completely in favor of local control and inertia. The majority of these articles call for a moderate approach. As an example, science as an academic discipline is summarized as follows: The science standards are not a national science curriculum or a federal mandate. They do not contain specifications for a national exam. They are not a set of rules, regulations, or approaches.

Standards are designed to move stakeholders in the following directions:

- Teaching the discipline for conceptual change
- Promoting integration of the discipline and other content areas
- Placing students in positions for them to see themselves as potential professionals and critical thinkers using specific content
- Providing a foundation for teachers to create experiences promoting inquiry, wonder, and understanding

Overall, most of the literature calls for the various standards to provide a frame of reference for judging the quality of specific content education that is already provided. In addition, and most important, the standards should be used as a tool that can serve and inspire the teacher.

Application

When structuring a semester or yearlong content experience for a class, there are only so many resources that can contribute to content and instructional practices. Some teachers turn to textbooks and their colleagues for concrete help in structuring day-to-day activities. They trust the textbook to cover the mandated content and colleagues to help provide the timeline or pace, choice of specific content, and related activities. Most of these choices are based on the resources available at the school and the department's institutionalized instructional inertia.

It is crucial that new teachers research and explore the various national frameworks, guidelines, and mandates. Specific guidelines, mandates, standards, and frameworks, provided by national content or curriculum organizations, filter through state and other bureaucratic agencies. Each state and district modifies and adapts these sources of guidance.

A quick search using various Internet search engines picked up too many "hits" to print. These sites feature a variety of content standards and guidelines in all content areas. After reading many content standards in science over the years, it's clear the overall usefulness of these documents has improved. It is fair to assume other content areas are also updating and becoming more valid and useful to teachers. In the past, rarely would any of these documents filter down to the school site and classroom teacher. Today, because of access to the Internet, they are available to everyone. So now, rather than turning to the textbook or colleagues first, a new teacher may treat himself or herself to a more global perspective on how teaching and learning should be experienced by teachers and students alike.

In the recent past, the information in these documents was limited to what a few thought should be taught. Authors of these documents have evolved their thinking and expanded their philosophy to present not only what should be taught but also how content should be taught, learned, and experienced by students. Most of them now include suggested content, delivery, and assessment strategies and standards. However, most don't give the teacher direct, concrete examples or activities ready for the classroom. They only suggest guidelines on how to create and construct a teacher's own experiences that are embedded in educational philosophy. If a new teacher is designing his or her own instructional strategies and activities, these types of documents are the best and most current sources of information available on a specific discipline. These articles can be interesting and motivating and should be visited and revisited in support of professional growth and inspiration.

Precautions and Possible Pitfalls

 Not all teachers keep current on the latest ideas in teaching and learning. Department or school politics can be a problem. Curricular leadership can come into play and conflict. The standards, mandates, guidelines, and frameworks can be interpreted in different ways, and philosophical differences could also be problematic. There is no way to predict how change will affect the relationships within a given school or department. Be aware that new teachers can become conflicted between philosophies when peer pressure is exerted. Help them become aware of the potential politics they could face when deciding what and how to teach.

Sources

Bell, M., & Rakow, S. (1998). Science and young children: The message from the National Science Education Standards. *Childhood Education, 74*(3), 164–167.
DeCarlo, C. (1998). Standards that serve you. *Instructor, 108*(4), 71.

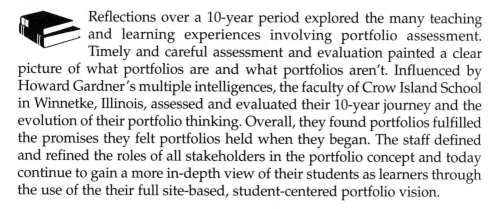

STRATEGY 36: Encourage beginning teachers to look beyond test scores to portfolios and a range of student work samples.

What the Research Says

Reflections over a 10-year period explored the many teaching and learning experiences involving portfolio assessment. Timely and careful assessment and evaluation painted a clear picture of what portfolios are and what portfolios aren't. Influenced by Howard Gardner's multiple intelligences, the faculty of Crow Island School in Winnetke, Illinois, assessed and evaluated their 10-year journey and the evolution of their portfolio thinking. Overall, they found portfolios fulfilled the promises they felt portfolios held when they began. The staff defined and refined the roles of all stakeholders in the portfolio concept and today continue to gain a more in-depth view of their students as learners through the use of the their full site-based, student-centered portfolio vision.

Application

 Mentors should discuss the following with new teachers when considering portfolios:

- Portfolios in education, by most definitions, are created to tell a story. Don't be too rigid when deciding what goes into one. Consider allowing and helping the students to decide what goes into the "story" of their learning and growth. Are the portfolios going to be teacher-centered or student-centered? Who decides what goes into one?
- Decide what work will go home and what should stay in the portfolio. Are parents presented a "chapter" at a time or are they presented a more temporal view within the portfolio paradigm?
- Whose portfolio is it? Should the teacher assume the role of a portfolio manager and let students decide what will counterbalance test scores and enter the portfolio? If teachers decide to do it this way, they will need to help the students in their decisions. The goal is developing competent and thoughtful storytellers. When students are first discovering what a portfolio is, they require a scaffolding strategy.
- Grading or attaching a letter grade to a portfolio seems to run contrary to the nature of the concept. Give it some thought.
- Select a time frame for the history of the learning a portfolio might represent. Is a portfolio a year's worth of work?
- For some students "telling" a long-term story is too abstract. Defining an audience for the work contributes to a more concrete picture.
- Attach meaning to each piece in a portfolio by asking students to write a short reason for its inclusion into the story. *Reflection tag* was the term used in the research literature. This contributes to the student's metacognitive growth and attaches further value and meaning to the individual content.
- Deliberately teach parents about the value of student portfolios: what they mean to teachers, the curriculum, and the students.

Precautions and Possible Pitfalls

Mentors should remind beginning teachers that on the surface, portfolios sound like a simple concept. They should not underestimate the learning curve for teachers, students, and parents if the concept is to really function at its best. Beginning teachers should expect some frustration during the implementation and transition to portfolio adoption. Mentors may need to remind new teachers that in this age of accountability testing, portfolios should be select examples of standards-based instruction.

Source

Hebert, E. (1998). Lessons learned about student portfolios. *Phi Delta Kappan, 79*(8), 583–585.

STRATEGY 37: Encourage beginning teachers to use ongoing evaluation techniques to enhance student learning.

What the Research Says

In a study of 12 elementary school teachers who were identified as "good" teachers by their peers, researchers documented the ongoing evaluation practices of 10 of these teachers who used continuous evaluative techniques to inform their practice working with special education students and diverse learners. Researchers noted that teachers who use ongoing evaluation in inclusive classrooms have a better idea of which students have mastered a concept, grasped a new pattern, or need the material presented in a different format (Alexandrin, 2003). The results of the focus group study yielded six main ideas:

1. Move around the classroom.

2. Observe student work frequently.

3. Have discussions with students.

4. View behaviors as indicators of understanding.

5. View teachers as not the sole problem solvers.

6. Have high expectations of all students.

Application

Often beginning teachers rely solely on test scores to evaluate their students' progress. By the time a unit test has been graded, it may be too late to intervene or reteach in context. Mentors may want to encourage the use of a "scan and plan" approach after beginning teachers deliver direct instruction and students are independently working. Beginning teachers should take the time to walk around the classroom as students begin independent assignments. By making a quick scan of student progress, noting how students are working, beginning teachers will notice if the same question comes up several times, or if students seem to be slowing at the same spot. They can then adjust their plans and quickly reteach that piece. Beginning teachers should check for understanding with questions that allow students to apply their learning, not just recite what they have heard.

Precautions and Possible Pitfalls

 Although some teachers like to use a tally sheet or narrative form to assess student progress as they circulate, mentors should avoid suggesting any labor-intensive system that takes more time than it saves in the long run.

Source

Alexandrin, J. R. (2003). Using continuous, constructive, classroom evaluations. *Teaching Exceptional Children, 36*(1), 52–58.

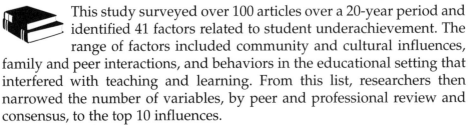

STRATEGY 38: Encourage beginning teachers to deepen their understanding of the wide range of specific factors associated with student underachievement.

What the Research Says

 This study surveyed over 100 articles over a 20-year period and identified 41 factors related to student underachievement. The range of factors included community and cultural influences, family and peer interactions, and behaviors in the educational setting that interfered with teaching and learning. From this list, researchers then narrowed the number of variables, by peer and professional review and consensus, to the top 10 influences.

The study focused its efforts on meeting the needs of diverse student populations in urban schools and then made research-based recommendations for school personnel. These recommendations or interventions included instructional strategies, methods of image building, and changes in the behaviors of academic professionals. Their goal was to be able to focus in on the key variables related to underachievement and to make specific recommendations for school personnel in assisting underachieving urban students.

Application

Most new teachers come from a background of success as students in the way they have experienced the institution of education. In fact, they liked it so much they wanted to be part of it and worked very hard to return to the classroom as teachers. From this perspective, teachers, especially new teachers, have a difficult time understanding why certain students don't feel the same way about the classroom, learning, and school as they do. Underachievement can be outside a new teacher's personal paradigm. Not understanding where an underachieving student is coming from frequently leads to teacher confusion, frustration, and avoidance of the student and the problem.

It is also common for many teachers, as they become more experienced and acquire a little political power within their school, to try to isolate themselves from underachieving students rather than try to work with them. However, with insight, reflection, empathy, and effort, they can gain some confidence in their ability to be successful with traditionally underachieving student groups. Information about the possible causes, along with a willingness to try to understand and create educational strategies can go a long way toward professional and personal fulfillment. From the research, a consensus of the 10 top influences, reviewed by experts in student underachievement and students at risk for failure, is listed here. All school personnel need to consider and act on these 10 top influences.

1. Teacher behavior refers to the teacher's actions that demonstrate care, respect, and interest in the personal, as well as academic, growth of their students.

2. Teacher expectations for students' achievement of realistic academic standards are directly or indirectly communicated to students and usually result in the students' attainment of those standards.

3. Curriculum relevance refers to the students' perceptions of how meaningful and usable the content material and the instructional methods are in their personal lives.

4. Class size is the number of students enrolled in a classroom.

5. Disengagement from school-related activities pertains to the lack of student involvement in and identification with the school community.

6. Confidence in the student's ability to achieve refers to the student's belief and expectation that he or she can learn academic material and be successful in school.

7. High mobility in school attendance or a student's transferring from one school to another can cause the student and his or her parents to feel alone and disconnected from the new school or school environment.

8. Parental expectations and involvement refers to the parents' realistic academic performance standards and goals for their children as well as their active engagement in meeting those goals.

9. Level of parents' education is the number of years parents have been involved in formal education as well as their level of academic accomplishments (e.g., high school graduation, bachelor's degree).

10. Poverty or low income (e.g., annual family income falling below poverty standards) often creates conditions in the family that, if uncorrected, could result in student underachievement.

While the study goes on to identify specific strategies to mitigate these influences, it concluded with three particularly noteworthy findings that emerged from threads connecting all 10 influences, which are summarized here:

• First, engagement level and expectations for success are critical not only for students but for school personnel and parents as well. The more confident all parties are in their ability to overcome barriers, the greater the chance for success. Past successes should be invoked as evidence that challenges can be overcome.

• Second, high mobility and attendance problems created learning and teaching environments characterized by disconnection and feelings of being alone. The effects of this relate to not only the students but also the parents and the school community as a whole. Schools can take positive steps to decrease the negative influence of mobility by inviting parents and students to become more involved and take a more active part in the school community.

• Third, school personnel have more influence over some conditions associated with chronic underachievement (e.g., teacher behaviors and expectations, curriculum relevance) than over others (e.g., low income of parents). The researchers found that school personnel could proactively address problems caused by some of the influences that they may not be able to control directly. Creating an environment where parents are included as vital members of the team was cited in numerous studies.

Most of the recommendations offered by the study involved a change in the strategies used by counselors, tutoring services, parent organizations, and caring teachers—systems already in place. All personnel need to use these traditional resources to address the common influences related to underachievement. Their study indicated that there was little need to develop new systems.

Precautions and Possible Pitfalls

No system or program will replace a single caring and involved teacher. This starts with one teacher dealing professionally and emotionally with one student at a time. This is done with the help, input, and insight of support services and other caring and insightful school personnel and the student's family. Also, be aware that not every family or family member will be useful in mitigating the student's problems. Some are the source of the problems.

It can't be emphasized enough that this is a team effort. Encourage your new teachers to gather all the information they can from others who know the student or students before acting. Make sure other experienced school personnel know what the teacher is doing and whom they are working with. This strategy can go a long way in helping new teachers avoid the potential pitfalls that are ingrained in student interventions.

Source

Arroyo, A., Rhoad, R., & Drew, P. (1999). Meeting diverse student needs in urban schools: Research-based recommendations for school improvement. *Preventing School Failure*, 43(4), 145–153.

 STRATEGY 39: As beginning teachers grade student writing assignments, encourage them to consider what students are able to do well before noting what needs improvement.

What the Research Says

In a review of current research, Gregg & Mather (2002) noted that there are many factors that influence the perception that a student is not a proficient writer. They propose that by considering writing skills (spelling, syntax, vocabulary, etc.) as well as the task format (dictated, copying, timed writing, etc.), teachers will discover a student's writing strengths and will also note areas that require support. They remind educators that it is vital to remember that writing is integrally related to social interactions and dialogue. In other words, writing is not simply the attempt to represent linguistic structures such as sentences, words, or phonemes; written expression requires a social process that is achieved through dialogue and interaction.

Application

Mentors should remind beginning teachers when teaching writing, to pay close attention to how the students perceive themselves as writers. Teachers should encourage the students to focus on finding and writing in their own unique voice. Beginning teachers should model the writing process, showing how ideas come first, then a rough draft to give them shape, followed by an editing process that addresses the mechanical aspects of the writing.

Mentors often have to discuss grading practices with beginning teachers who may struggle with consistency. When grading writing assignments, beginning teachers should consider grading the first draft for content only, engaging the student in a written dialogue of what he or she is saying in his or her writing. Mentors should advise that beginning teachers quell their urges to point out paragraphing, capitalization, and spelling errors as they read. They can demonstrate the difference between content and mechanics by isolating them in their teaching and evaluation process.

Experienced teachers recognize that writing skill occurs on a developmental continuum and they help their students to see individual growth along that continuum. They understand that students with disabilities often view writing as a hated task, and as standards move toward embedding writing in more curricular areas, poor writing skills can lead to a broader dislike of school in general. Writing itself is a very personal enterprise, and for a student who struggles with it, writing can be a very personal failure. Mentors may need to remind beginning teachers that students who understand that what they have to say is unique and valuable are much more open to risking committing their thoughts to paper. They know that the mechanical facets of writing can be addressed concretely farther along in the writing process.

Precautions and Possible Pitfalls

 In recent years many teachers and parents have lamented the lack of spelling and grammar instruction in schools. Beginning teachers are often at a loss as to how to incorporate these aspects of English into their instruction of literature. Mentors can help beginning teachers plan how to address the principles behind common spelling patterns as well as the basic grammatical components of standard written English for their students. Most students learn these rules more effectively in context, so beginning teachers should consider embedding a lesson on a specific rule of grammar by asking the students to correct it or apply it in their own writing.

Sources

Gregg, N., & Mather, N. (2002). School is fun at recess. *Journal of Learning Disabilities, 35*(1), 7–23.

6

Supporting New Teachers as They Develop Personal Teaching Styles and Time Management Strategies

It's what you learn after you know it all that counts.

John Wooden

 STRATEGY 40: Insist that beginning teachers post an agenda before the start of class.

What the Research Says

Using an agenda of the day's lesson makes learning more relevant to students and takes the mystery out of what is going to be covered in class that day. An agenda also helps keep the teacher organized with regard to the information to be learned. An agenda that includes the lesson outline on the board or an overhead transparency can arouse students' thinking about the various topics and help them connect to prior knowledge about those topics. A connection between knowledge already known and new knowledge is a critical component of meaningful learning.

Based on Ausubel's (1960) theory of how knowledge is structured, the most meaningful learning is dependent upon a lesson's material being organized in a way that "connects" and makes it meaningful to the learner. The student needs to be able to connect the information being taught with ideas, concepts, and examples that are already present in the learner's cognitive structure. According to Ausubel, the framework of a preorganized agenda provides a stable sequential structure that students can use as a framework to build upon the objective of the lesson. It prepares students in advance for what is to come, tells students how the teacher has organized the material, and makes the material to be received more meaningful. This process is what Ausubel calls *meaningful reception learning*.

Application

Who remembers being in a class and having no idea what was going to be covered that day, whether or not a test was imminent, or if the teacher would assign a hefty homework assignment over a holiday weekend? Most students have had this experience more than once. The use of the board or an overhead transparency covering the day's agenda can serve a number of purposes. The agenda should be posted at the beginning of class, preferably as students are entering the classroom. Students then know in advance what is to come. It can also cut down or eliminate the number of "What are we going to do today?" questions teachers frequently encounter. There are no surprises about an upcoming assignment, a concept being taught that day, test dates, or homework assignments. The skilled mentor knows the value of posting an agenda in terms of saving time answering students' questions. The beginning teacher may see this at first as just another task that takes time and may not realize the significance in terms of organization and pacing. In addition, using an agenda places the onus of responsibility on the students for keeping a record of what material is to be covered, not only for themselves but also for students who are absent.

Schools that use block scheduling, where students attend class every other day, can benefit even more by not having to wait two days before

Figure 6.1   Sample Agenda

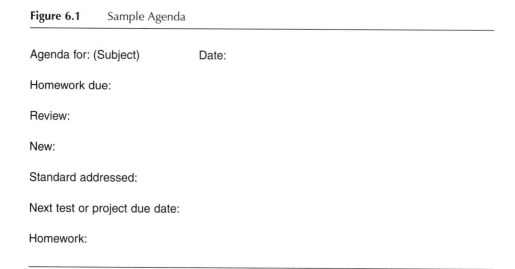

Agenda for: (Subject)   Date:

Homework due:

Review:

New:

Standard addressed:

Next test or project due date:

Homework:

catching up. The student merely calls his or her homework buddy, who checks the agenda he or she wrote down that day. The use of an agenda can alleviate miscommunication problems ("I didn't know we were having a test today") and can reduce the academic stress some students feel while trying to juggle and organize homework, projects, tests, and so on. A sample agenda might include the information shown in Figure 6.1.

The teacher can easily create these agendas as a computer presentation software slide (e.g., using PowerPoint), and a record is then kept for future planning. Beginning teachers report that these agendas help in reflecting over a lesson and in the planning of future ones. In many schools across the country principals are requiring teachers to post the standards they are teaching. By doing this as part of the daily agenda, the teacher, students, and administration are all on the same page with regard to standards. Agendas can help the accountability for all concerned.

The use of this type of agenda helps keep the teacher focused on the lesson and leaves no secrets for the student about what will be covered that day. By using an overhead transparency, teachers who are assigned to multiple classrooms (not uncommon for a new teacher) are able to take the agenda with them and not waste valuable time rewriting the day's activities in each room. After a lesson, the teacher can use the agenda to make notes about pacing, transitions, and lesson evaluations to be used in subsequent years.

Precautions and Possible Pitfalls

 The agenda should not be a detailed outline of each facet of the lesson, but rather a general outline of the day's activities. When students set about copying detailed agendas into notes, their focus turns to note taking, and the teacher risks losing their attention. In addition, agendas should include enough information to pique the student's interest about the day's lesson but not be so detailed that they become meaningless notes. Copying the agenda should take the student no more than two to three minutes at the beginning of class (allowing the teacher to take attendance, speak with a student, etc.).

Source

Ausubel, D. (1960). The use of advance organizers in the learning and retention of meaningful verbal learning. *Journal of Educational Psychology, 51*, 267–272.

 STRATEGY 41: Help beginning teachers manage the special challenges within block scheduling.

What the Research Says

The purpose of this study was to examine the experiences of new teachers as they negotiated the beginnings of their careers in less traditional schedules. In this case a new teacher was described as a teacher less than three months out of a teacher preparation program. The study lasted one calendar year and included 31 first-year teachers. Data were collected from these teachers in three urban school districts that had high schools offering a 4 × 4 block schedule. Data were collected from the first-year teachers only and did not include administrators, master teachers, or other support staff.

Three areas emerged as problematic:

- Adjusting instruction to extended class period formats
- Transitioning learning activities
- Assessing student progress

In the adjustment category, the problems identified included managing class time, varying instruction throughout the class period, running out of materials or activities before the end of class, and relying on only a single instructional method. Many fell into patterns of worksheets or end of chapter questions, long lectures, or letting students do homework to keep them quiet until the bell. First-year teachers were not prepared to vary instructional strategies or make transitions. Some resorted to college-type teaching, heavy on notes and lecture.

Transition periods from one activity to another, utilizing a variety of instructional strategies that are desirable in a block format, became a sticking point for new teachers. Maintaining a learning environment and climate became difficult and students "messed around too much" or saw it as a time to misbehave. Because of this, new teachers often avoided transition periods and used only limited numbers of instructional strategies.

Teachers in the study often reported being very uncomfortable with students out of their seats or moving around. "Losing control" became a very limiting fear in the creation of learning environments.

This fear also limited assessment strategies and tactics. Many new teachers found pencil and paper tests could not adequately assess gains in student learning. Yet, performance assessments were rare because of, again, the fear of losing control. Thus "seat work" became the norm. Socratic seminars, cooperative learning strategies, simulations, role-playing, and laboratory or work-station strategies presented management problems that most new teachers were not equipped to deal with. New teachers often had problems knowing how much value or weight to place on more authentic assessments and "doing" types of activities. They did not realize that alternative forms of assessment could be quantified by criteria matched to learning objectives through rubrics.

Longer class periods require careful, structured planning, utilization of a variety of instructional methods, and diverse assessment practices to maximize the potential they offer. New teachers "on the block" and especially first-year teachers had problems fully developing skills in these areas. The study also found that if the staff-development opportunities were beyond the range of the first-year teachers, learning advanced techniques created frustration for the teachers that transferred to the classroom.

Application

If the new teacher is new to a block schedule format, mentors should consider the results of this study. What seems natural to them may be a trial by fire for a new teacher. Most, if not all, schools that utilize a block or modified block schedule also favor a student-centered curricular approach to student learning or pedagogy. It is also clear new teachers often encounter discipline and management problems when students leave their seats and class periods are longer. Unfortunately, experience is often the best teacher. For new teachers, their student-teaching experience might have been very different from what they may be facing in their first teaching position. So what can a new teacher do and what can mentors tell them?

There are many terms within educational jargon that describe teaching and learning arrangements better suited for the longer time frames typical of block schedules. The concepts of problem-based, theme-based, student-centered, or activity and discovery learning ask students to take a more active role in their own learning. Teachers facilitate or orchestrate learning rather than dictate it. Ted Sizer's (of Brown University) Coalition of Essential Schools philosophy sees the student as a worker and the teacher as a facilitator. The point here is that students are required to take a more proactive role in their own learning, when they need to know things, and what they need to know. These types of teaching and learning arrangements also require the students to learn a new role and teachers to teach students their new role. Many students have not learned to self-regulate in classrooms that teach in a student-centered manner.

Successful student-centered classroom environments in block formats often look chaotic but are actually highly planned and organized chaos. The most important idea to keep in mind is to teach students to learn in these new settings. Most kids coming from the "stand-and-deliver" experience are not equipped to deal with the new expectations in longer classes. So between new teachers' inexperience and student inexperience, all must realize that it will require time, usually a semester to a year, for both the new teacher and the students to adjust.

Teachers can help themselves by learning all they can about how to create, manage, and assess and evaluate activity-based classes (typical of block schedules) and activities. Every activity and expected student or curricular outcome needs to be broken down into smaller manageable units with built-in student accountability at each step along the way. How small the teacher makes these subunits depends on the maturity and educational needs of the students being managed. The pace of instruction needs to be flexible, and the teacher needs to expect to make adjustments on the fly as the students give clues that they're not getting it or as the teacher runs into curricular roadblocks. Every student moves at a different pace.

When administrators come into a class, the teacher needs to be accountable. Teachers should be prepared to tout their latest student-based activity and show the administrator how they manage the learning that is taking place. Have an administrator shadow an activity or a student through that activity. Any administrator in a block schedule type school knows what the teacher is up against and can often offer help or direct the new teacher to a teacher that could be helpful. The sooner the administrator sees that the new teacher is engaged in trying to make the best of his or her schedule, the sooner the teacher will receive support.

Precautions and Possible Pitfalls

Student-centered learning and block scheduling do not mean a teacher needs to abandon all stand-and-deliver or other more traditional techniques. To completely abandon techniques a teacher is experienced with or has learned in favor of a whole new set of methods is a ticket for frustration and potential disaster. Teachers should plan to step out of their comfort zone, but not completely. Planning short-term units, utilizing unfamiliar strategies, acclimating slowly, and tinkering and modifying as you go may be more effective with a new teacher. Eventually new teaching and learning methods will take over or blend with the teacher's existing methods. Again, teachers are learning on their feet, and this takes time.

If a new teacher is trying another teacher's strategy or activity, he or she should expect to need to modify it to fit his or her own comfort zone. And finally, stepping into a new position needs to be seen as a work in progress. A teacher should plan full acclimation as a two- or three-year experience.

Source

Zepeda, S. J., & Mayers, R. S. (2001, April/May). New kids on the block: Beginning teachers face challenges. *High School Journal, 84*(4) 1–11.

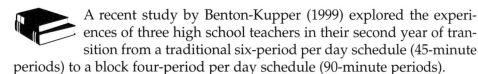

STRATEGY 42: *Ensure that beginning teachers use a variety of instructional strategies.*

What the Research Says

 A recent study by Benton-Kupper (1999) explored the experiences of three high school teachers in their second year of transition from a traditional six-period per day schedule (45-minute periods) to a block four-period per day schedule (90-minute periods).

Their findings suggest the block schedule provided more opportunities than the traditional six-period day for instructional strategies that actively engage the students in learning. The additional time provided in a double period allows teachers to provide more depth of content within their classrooms through discussion, projects, and instructional materials.

Application

For middle and secondary schools across the nation utilizing some type of block scheduling (four 90-minute periods per day, or three 120-minute periods per day, with classes meeting every other day), the opportunities abound for teachers to work individually with students, go deeply into the content, and assess the students' individual learning styles. Teachers at schools where the block schedule has been implemented for many years report that the schedule increases their ability to know where students are in terms of learning the content. This knowledge allows the teacher to plan and instruct lessons that will lead to student success (Buckman, King, & Ryan, 1995).

However, teachers new to longer time frames sometimes experience "planning shock." Planning for longer time frames can present challenges. Help those new to the "block" see the possibilities.

In a block period there is a tendency for the flow of the lesson to be less disjointed than in a traditional format. Having extended time in a block gives teachers the opportunity to construct a full lesson, introduce a topic or concept, discuss it, and bring that topic to closure all within one class period. Teachers may also find more time in the block schedule to develop difficult key concepts.

In a Southern California high school that has had block scheduling (120-minute periods every other day) for over 25 years, even new teachers find the opportunities to provide a wide range of instructional strategies within a lesson intended to increase students' interest, knowledge, and success. For example, in one class the teacher was able to review for a test, provide direct instruction, have cooperative learning groups, view a video followed by time for a class discussion, and begin individual project presentations, all within the same class period. To be able to cover all of these instructional strategies in a traditional class period would be impossible.

The extended time frame of block scheduling also allows time for activities implementing multiple intelligences that might be more difficult in a non-block setting. Teachers also report that with block scheduling there are more opportunities for in-depth reading of literature and class discussions that might not otherwise happen given the relatively short 45-minute period. Without this additional time, more work must be assigned as homework, which does not give students the advantage of having the teacher as a facilitator.

Precautions and Possible Pitfalls

New teachers may, at first, be intimidated by the extended time of block scheduling. Their practice in the planning of lessons may be limited to single periods. Concerns about filling the time with worthwhile activities may abound. If they don't have experience in planning for the block, they should consult a trusted colleague or mentor for help in lesson planning. Block scheduling requires a unique perspective. The primary consideration should be to keep students engaged. This can be accomplished by changing activities or focus about every 20 minutes for high energy students or extend the time frame for more mature students. If students are given the opportunity to experience multiple methods of grasping information, their interest level will be high. The greatest mistake a teacher new to block scheduling can make is to think that lesson planning simply means putting two single-period lessons together. The worst use of the block is for the teacher to present a lecture or lecture-based instruction for the entire class period.

Sources

Benton-Kupper, J. (1999, October). Teaching in the block: Perceptions from within. *High School Journal, 83*(1), 26.
Buckman, D., King, B., & Ryan, S. (1995). Block scheduling: A means to improving school climate. *NASSP Bulletin, 79*(571), 9–18.

 STRATEGY 43: Remind beginning teachers that improving personal organization has a positive impact on student achievement.

What the Research Says

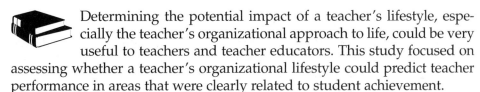 Determining the potential impact of a teacher's lifestyle, especially the teacher's organizational approach to life, could be very useful to teachers and teacher educators. This study focused on assessing whether a teacher's organizational lifestyle could predict teacher performance in areas that were clearly related to student achievement.

The study was conducted at a comprehensive southeastern state university. Seventy-five students, who were engaged in student teaching in a variety of public school settings ranging from kindergarten through high school, took part in this study. Five university supervisors, with an average of 15 student teachers assigned to each, also participated in the research. Of the student participants, 52 were male and 23 were female.

Each teacher subject was given a Life Style Approach Inventory to assess organizational style and self-management. They were also given the Teacher Performance Appraisal Instrument as a measure of teacher behaviors that have been found in research literature to be positively correlated with student achievement.

The researchers concluded that student teachers who reported being the most and least organized also tended to receive the highest and lowest ratings for their teaching performance. It was also suggested that higher scores on the Life Style Approach Inventory were also positively associated with life satisfaction, self-efficacy, optimism, and positive health, and lower scores were associated with stress and poor health.

Application

 Many new teachers cite a variety of factors *other than themselves* that contribute to the difficulties of schools. In a second survey of attitudes toward public schools, teachers cited lack of parental interest, lack of proper financial support, lack of student interest, and lack of discipline as being the biggest problems facing public schools. However, mentors know that much of what happens and is accomplished in the classroom is a product of the teacher's performance.

New teachers bring with them an organizational lifestyle approach that affects their performance and probably the achievement of their students. Those who have a clear focus on what they want to achieve and an effective time-management style in completing tasks support pathways toward achievement and bring an organized approach that is reflected in their teaching behaviors. Achieving an organized lifestyle will influence teaching performance, and those scoring highest on the Life Style Approach Inventory were also most likely to believe their behaviors influence performance. Mentors can facilitate a discussion of personal organizational styles by sharing their own techniques and how they developed them.

Precautions and Possible Pitfalls

This thinking and reflection should not be used to predict a person's aptitude for teaching. Like flaws in sports techniques, it should be used to analyze flaws in teaching techniques that don't contribute to student achievement and teacher well-being. It also supports a view of the teacher assuming responsibility for the classroom outcomes rather than exporting the responsibility to other factors.

Source

Long, J. D., & Gaynor, P. (1993). Organizational life style as a predictor of student teaching performance. *Education, 113*(3), 2–5.

 STRATEGY 44: Encourage beginning teachers to not let everyday activities obscure class goals and long-term objectives.

What the Research Says

Student assessment through portfolios is becoming popular. However, there is little guidance for the creation of portfolios in some disciplines. One model involved a record of individual student goals and objectives and whether they were achieved, a record of student grades, a self-evaluation form, and work samples within a high school chemistry class. This portfolio model demonstrates student progression while also engaging students in personal reflection on their class experiences and learning processes. The research found that student responses at teacher-student conferences dealing with personal goals and objectives have been positive and much of the subjectivity is avoided.

Application

A standards-based portfolio of this type seems like a logical extension of the rubric or class syllabus philosophy. The main question here is who develops the balance between a teacher-centered or student-centered approach to goal and objective creation? Mentors should advise new teachers to consider the creation of a class-designed portfolio facilitated and managed collaboratively. Teachers have certain content standards and process requirements based on school, state, and national expectations for performance. The major goals of constructing a portfolio of this type are to clearly illustrate and communicate the goals of instruction and engage students in self-assessment.

Ideally, the students' goals will be combined with the teacher-mandated goals. Student goals might feature class-generated, more personal goals that form a student-centered working guideline shared by all stakeholders. This might consider and include the academic side as well as a more metacognitive side.

Once agreed upon, the portfolio (rubric or syllabus format) document becomes a class academic guide that students, teachers, and parents can relate to, visit, and revisit as needed to discover where they are on the educational map within the class.

New teachers may need assistance developing their own curricular guides for a period of time within the class to help students keep clear goals in mind for themselves as they acquire discipline knowledge and process skills. Teacher-student conferences can help teachers and students mutually assess progress. New teachers should consider doing a partial guide-rubric-syllabus and have the students add their own personal goals and objectives to help them define the type of literacy they hope to achieve. Theirs could end up looking very different from the teacher's. It would be interesting to have students do this at the beginning of a class to help get a feel for their expectations for teaching and learning in class.

Precautions and Possible Pitfalls

Mentors may need to share that portfolios have a way of becoming obsolete as class conditions change. New teachers need to be prepared to revisit the portfolio framework as needed. Adjustments will most likely need to be made, and new teachers should be prepared to share the responsibility for this as needed. Goals and objectives that seem feasible early may need to be mediated. Experience over time will help the process evolve, and the comfort level with this assessment tool will increase.

Sources

Adamchik, C. (1996). The design and assessment of chemistry portfolios. *Journal of Chemical Education, 73*(6), 528–530.

Hebert, E. (1998). Lessons learned about student portfolios. *Phi Delta Kappan, 79*(8), 583–585.

 STRATEGY 45: Assist beginning teachers in looking behind the scenes to establish context when assessing the teaching styles of others.

What the Research Says

 Once leaving the confines of a college or university classroom, new teachers are often confronted with a range of teaching styles that they may not be familiar with. This can be a confusing time, as many times the college or university programs have defined teaching styles and techniques that are deemed the "correct" way to teach and may be very different from what a new teacher is confronted with in the real world.

This article (Black & Davern, 1998) describes scenarios where new teachers were confronted with confusing classroom situations that became so distracting that the new teacher failed to see the innovative aspects of the particular classroom. The article goes further to describe a communication breakdown that begins with new teachers failing to ask host teachers questions that would have helped them to see the "method behind the madness" in what they were observing and experiencing, usually for the first time.

For example, it is very common to see problem-based pedagogy or discovery learning techniques in classrooms these days. Kids are out of their seats, working in teams, and the noise level can be high. To a novice it can look like nothing constructive is taking place, yet to a veteran teacher it is a controlled and orchestrated teaching and learning environment. Various teaching strategies can be seen in such classrooms such as cooperative grouping, sophisticated teaming skills, mutual learning, learning self-regulatory skills, self-pacing, and competitive strategies. Yes, students are out of their seats and not all the students seem to be engaged, but the majority of them are engaged. Having students sitting quietly at their desks doesn't ensure everyone is on task either. University supervisors critiqued the scenarios that were used in the research to show how novice teachers could easily misread valid learning and teaching strategies.

Application

If teachers are going to take the time to visit a classroom and observe, they should be clear on how to make the most of the experience. Careful analysis of the overall character of a class activity, lesson, or strategy can help new teachers focus on the details. Don't let their first impressions define what is going on. List their questions and analyze them as best you can and be ready to discuss them with the classroom teacher. Critiquing teaching practices is a skill in itself and needs to be learned. It will become a valuable skill. Ultimately it is important to make distinctions between those practices they would use and incorporate into their own repertoire and those they would not.

Without appearing judgmental, mentors should instruct new teachers to ask the teacher or teachers involved why he or she chose a specific teaching strategy. Once they become aware of possibly new perspectives, they become free to learn from them and to apply them to their own instructional practices.

Share the strategies for successful observations that include the following:

• Have them listen carefully to the concerns of the teacher they are observing. Suggest they practice presenting a message to them that indicates they are interested and want to discuss issues freely, nonjudgmentally, constructively, and openly.

• Help them model respect and appreciation for the challenges that school staff experience. Suggest that they go behind the instructional scenes and ask what the teacher educator needed to do before the observation and what resources were needed to get to this point in time with the students.

• Have them explore the teacher's perceptions of the needs of the class to help validate what is happening in the classroom. Explore the strengths and weaknesses of the strategies used.

• Suggest that they communicate their own teaching practices and philosophies to veteran teachers. Have them practice skillful ways of raising difficult subjects. Realize differences are inevitable within any staff. Nurture their spirit of independent thought and learn to diplomatically raise differences they may have regarding practices and philosophies.

Help them develop a critical analytic ability and reflective skills to help identify, explore, and articulate your ideas.

Precautions and Possible Pitfalls

As most mentors know, some veteran teachers may not be as receptive to questioning and visitors as others. Make sure new teachers don't take it personally. Hopefully all their contacts will be positive and useful. As with any profession, there is a range of competency among teachers, and not every contact they make may click. Also, teachers are not "good" or "bad" all the time. They have good and bad days, successful and not so successful lessons. Classes of students can also have bad days when nothing seems to work. Proms, dances, Fridays, Mondays, sporting events, weather, and a range of other factors can affect a specific lesson or observation on any given day.

Source

Black, A., & Davern, L. (1998). When a preservice teacher meets the classroom team (managing conflicts of teacher strategies). *Educational Leadership, 55*(5), 55.

STRATEGY 46: Remind beginning teachers to become classroom managers before becoming content specialists.

What the Research Says

Teacher planning refers to the wide variety of instructional decisions teachers make prior to the execution of plans during teaching. Some of the key factors found to affect planning practices include students, curriculum materials, teacher guides, and the physical facilities. In the student realm, ability level, gender, amount of class participation, student self-concepts, social competence, and work habits contribute to many other planning considerations. Curriculum materials influence decisions based on the quality or quantity of textbooks and support materials. The physical facilities include room size and a variety of other related school characteristics that include the all-important school schedule. The goals of the administration, site administrators, and school and department policies also add to the many considerations teachers face. To these external forces add the teacher's own interests, subject matter specialty, and experience.

This study (Sardo-Brown, 1996) looked into the literature and found few studies that looked at novice teacher planning. Sardo-Brown's study looked at how two first-year teachers planned their first and second years of teaching and compared and contrasted the differences between the years. The two teachers in the study were selected based on their competency within their graduating education classes and because both had obtained employment in secondary schools right out of teacher education.

Some of the most noticeable findings between first- and second-year planning include

- For the most part, new teachers did not plan to emphasize content during the early weeks of school but considered management issues a higher priority.
- Both second-year novices dedicated much more time to how to set up and teach rules, procedures, and class structure along with how to develop early rapport with their students.
- The teachers moved further away in time and reference from their student-teaching experiences where rules were routinized and planning was rule bound.
- In the second year, they were more receptive to new ideas and inservicing.
- Both planned major adjustments to their methods of assessment. Both sought out more time-efficient strategies and planned to use more high-level assessment strategies as learning devices.
- Both novices in this study married between their first and second years and looked for new ways to get more leisure time. Both credited their marriages for growing confidence in themselves as teachers and both felt "older."
- In the second year, they tried to do more of their planning at school.
- Both viewed the area of assessment as a major concern and planned numerous changes in their second year. They felt they were not prepared to successfully tackle assessment in their first year.
- Both felt more comfortable planning in their second year.
- Both continued to struggle with the problem of reconciling their own beliefs about their teaching with the incongruent beliefs of the principal and other colleagues.
- They both had a greater awareness of the cognitive and emotional needs of their students.

Application

 It is clear from the research that preservice teachers move from being content specialists and borrowers of instructional tactics to educators and instructional strategists their second year and thereafter.

First-year teachers often don't know what they don't know until experience becomes their teacher. The tactic derived from the research becomes being able to learn from what teachers see in front of them rather than from what someone tells them.

New teachers should develop their own analytical skills as they implement a "best guess" instructional plan. Teachers need to do the "science" it takes to determine what happens when real students meet a teacher's management and instructional strategy. Seeing everything a new teacher does as a work in progress will be comforting. Keep in mind that a teaching style is something a new teacher will find in himself or herself and not something that is learned. The classroom experience is like the game on Friday night. It tells teachers what they need to work on the following week.

Teachers will do well to also remember they are standing on the shoulders of those that came before, and they all went through similar experiences. How a beginning teacher views himself or herself as a teacher should not be based solely on early efforts. It should be based on how a teacher responds to his or her experiences with effort and reflection and how resilient and adaptive he or she can be. Analyze those problems, adjust, and move on.

Precautions and Possible Pitfalls

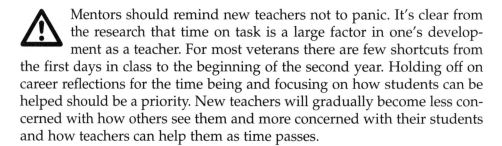 Mentors should remind new teachers not to panic. It's clear from the research that time on task is a large factor in one's development as a teacher. For most veterans there are few shortcuts from the first days in class to the beginning of the second year. Holding off on career reflections for the time being and focusing on how students can be helped should be a priority. New teachers will gradually become less concerned with how others see them and more concerned with their students and how teachers can help them as time passes.

Source

Sardo-Brown, D. (1996). A longitudinal study of novice secondary teachers' planning: Year two. *Teaching & Teacher Education, 12*(5), 519–530.

7

Supporting
New Teachers
as They Develop
a Variety of
Strategies for
Helping At-Risk
and Special
Needs Students
Succeed

You cannot put the same shoe on every foot.

Syrus Publius

STRATEGY 47: *Encourage beginning teachers to use a "hypothesis and frequent reflection" strategy when working with students who have special education needs.*

What the Research Says

In an analysis of 19 expert special educators, Stough and Palmer (2003) determined that the success of these teachers and their students with special needs could be attributed to their unique approach and application of pedagogical knowledge. The central finding of this study was that each teacher was concerned about individual student performance.

These teachers had a minimum of five years' experience and were evaluated using a multifaceted approach (interviewing, videotaping, observation, stimulated recall, and field notes). The study was conducted in five schools ranging from urban to rural and elementary through high school levels. In addition, the special education needs of the students varied along the continuum of services (RSP, MM, ED, etc.).

Considering first the academic behavior, then the classroom behavior, each teacher used a hypothesis/reflection strategy to teach his or her students. By using their prior knowledge of the individual student, each teacher would develop a hypothesis about the student and then an instructional plan to meet those individual needs. During the instruction, the teacher would assess the individual student's progress and reflect on the efficacy of the practice in that moment, making any needed adjustments. The teachers believed strongly that all students could learn and were collectively working to increase student independence and emotional well-being.

Application

Beginning teachers will benefit from taking the time to review available data (individual education program [IEP], 504, cumulative file, etc.) to develop a basic profile of specific students and their individual strengths and weaknesses. Using background pedagogical knowledge of instructional practice, the mentor and beginning teacher can work together to form a hypothesis about how each student will benefit most from specific instruction. As the instruction unfolds, the beginning teacher should note the student's response and can adjust the practice as needed.

Mentors may want to remind their beginning teachers that often, by considering the needs of one student, teachers can positively impact an entire class. For example, if beginning teachers notice that individual students need to have written directions read aloud due to a processing delay, they may discover that the entire class performs better when the instructions are reviewed orally with the whole class prior to beginning an assignment.

Frequent reflection is the key to evaluating the hypothesis and determining the efficacy of instructional practice. Mentors may need to guide their beginning teachers through this process until they become proficient. With time and experience, beginning teachers' knowledge of student characteristics will increase, as will the number of instructional strategies they are able to employ.

Precautions and Possible Pitfalls

It is important that mentors ensure that beginning teachers form their hypotheses about individual students based on facts or observable behaviors. It can be tempting to assume that because a student has the same disability as another student, their instructional needs are the same. The key to excellence in teaching students with special needs is to consider each student individually. It can also be tempting to do what has always been done rather design a practice that specifically meets an individual's needs. By constructively using assessment and subsequent reflection to inform their practice, beginning teachers can accelerate their students' success.

Source

Stough, L. M., & Palmer, D. (2003). Special thinking in special settings: A qualitative study of expert special educators. *Journal of Special Education, 36*(4), 206–223.

STRATEGY 48: *Advise beginning teachers to prepare general education students with instructional strategies prior to forming cooperative groups that include students with disabilities.*

What the Research Says

A study was conducted to assess the efficacy of cooperative learning groups for students with autism (Kamps et al., 2002). The study included a control group with no specific peer interaction, a cooperative group with specific learning objectives, and a social skills group with fewer formal guidelines. Student attention was measured over the course of a year, and the results showed a significant increase in attention and social skills acquisition in both the social skills group and the cooperative group. The target students increased their attention from below 30 seconds to over 191 seconds measured in 5-minute probes. In addition, the students in the social skills group and the cooperative group increased their interactions with others more than three times the baseline. The researchers determined that the efficacy increased when the peers were trained in effective instructional strategies. Understanding modeling, reinforcement, visual cuing, scripts, and natural settings significantly contributed to student success.

Application

Cooperative groupings can be an effective way to vary instructional approach, but many beginning teachers lack the experience to ensure that student groups are effective learning opportunities rather than management issues. Beginning teachers should be encouraged to carefully consider the goal of the group activity and the skills required to ensure success prior to including group activities in their lesson plans. Mentors should emphasize the importance of teaching process before content and advise beginning teachers that teaching students directly about group roles and group process will enhance any group experience.

When student groups include students with disabilities, beginning teachers should take more time to consider the specific expectations for the activity. General education students who are aware of basic teaching techniques such as modeling, reinforcement, and visual cuing will be able to employ these strategies when working with their peers with disabilities. Beginning teachers should model these teaching strategies with their students in the large group prior to breaking students into smaller groups.

Precautions and Possible Pitfalls

Mentors need to warn beginning teachers not to rely too heavily on a capable and compassionate student to be the constant helper for a student with a disability. By teaching instructional strategies to all of the students, a beginning teacher can widen the support network for the student with a disability.

Source

Kamps, D., Potucek, J., Dugan, E., Kravitz, T., Gonzalez-Lopez, A., Garcia, J., Carnazzo, K., Morrison, L., & Kane, L. G. (2002). Peer training to facilitate social interaction for elementary students with autism and their peers. *Exceptional Children, 68*(2),173–188.

 STRATEGY 49: *Encourage beginning teachers to be creative in designing ways to support and challenge students with severe disabilities who are included in general education classrooms.*

What the Research Says

Although many students with learning disabilities are successfully included in general education classes for both academic and social growth, frequently IEP teams limit their expectations of students with severe disabilities. Most students with severe disabilities are placed primarily for social goals, and any academic expectation is limited to the life skill training that occurs in the special education classroom (Downing & Eichinger, 2003). Creative teachers can identify a myriad of ways to assist students with severe disabilities to work on their academic goals. Use of pictorial charts and number cards can provide a bridge for students. Downing and Echinger offer the example of a student in a biology class who sorts and counts seeds while nondisabled peers identify the genus. When the class is working on writing a story, the student with a severe disability might select pictures that would illustrate the story. Students who are learning how to follow directions and interact socially might be called on to distribute papers or collect homework routinely. The researchers offer additional suggestions for teachers who use random groupings of students for specific activities. Students with severe disabilities could use pictures of the class and a die to place students into envelopes forming groups (with the assistance of a paraeducator) while the teacher is delivering the lecture.

Applications

Often beginning teachers are intimidated by the significant needs of a student with severe disabilities. Beginning teachers need encouragement to develop reasonable and appropriate lessons for students who have special needs. The mentor should assist the teacher in taking the first step by considering the student's IEP goals together. With those goals in mind, the next step is to open a dialogue regarding the specific curriculum as well as the classroom procedures of the specific class. Mentors may find it helpful to create a chart that blocks out the basics of these two areas so they can be viewed simultaneously to begin the planning process. Either viewing the chart or simply reviewing the IEP and lesson plan book, the beginning teacher can consider the cross-over points that could be avenues for appropriate learning activities for the student. Mentors may point out classroom procedures—particularly routines for homework turn-in, group activities, lectures versus labs, etc. If the beginning teacher is invited to look for opportunities for the student to practice his or her academic goals (writing name, recognizing routines, etc.), some ideas will arise. Beginning teachers should then consider the essential standards that are being addressed by the specific unit and what level of modification is appropriate for the specific student.

Precautions and Possible Pitfalls

 Beginning teachers are often intimidated and worry about judgment when other adults are in the classroom. If a student has the services of a paraeducator during the general education class, the beginning teacher may benefit from the mentor's facilitation of a three-way meeting to ensure that the paraeducator is aware of both the curricular and individual student's goals for the lesson as well as the teacher's instructional style.

Mentors should help beginning teachers avoid contrived matches of curriculum and academic goals. The more real and relevant the activity is, the more likely it is to benefit the student's growth overall. Mentors may need to point out that while making a collage of food groups might be appropriate for a nutrition or biology class, it wouldn't be appropriate for history.

Source

Downing, J. E., & Eichinger, J. (2003). Creating learning opportunities for students with severe disabilities in inclusive classrooms, *Teaching Exceptional Children, 36*(1), 26–32.

 STRATEGY 50: Encourage beginning teachers to use a reflective narrative model to facilitate behavior modification decisions.

What the Research Says

In an effort to move teachers from a reactive behavior modification approach to a proactive model, graduate students at the College of New Jersey were asked to use an adapted narrative model to focus on behavior changes for students with problem behaviors (Rao et al., 2003). The narrative model used was broken into two parts. The first half was devoted to the observation of the behavior including items such as antecedents, behavior, and consequences. The second half was devoted to reflections on the part of the teacher. Teachers were encouraged to write down their thoughts regarding the behavior and the efficacy of any intervention attempted.

Some of the advantages of the narrative log were the empathy they elicited from the teachers. By viewing the behaviors as a means for students rather than just trying to extinguish them, the teachers felt a greater sense of understanding. Likewise, the narrative lent itself to placing the behaviors in the context of the curriculum. Teachers were able to focus on the skills required for the specific academic task and draw conclusions from that angle. Environmental issues that may have been contributing to negative behaviors were noted. The reflective format encouraged teachers to focus on specific behaviors. Lastly, the reflective nature of this approach invited teachers to contemplate their own feelings about the specific behaviors.

Application

Many induction programs feature the "plan, teach, reflect, apply" approach to curriculum design, yet few beginning teachers are able to independently take advantage of the value of reflection when it comes to behavior management. Teacher education classes cover basic behavior management techniques by advising teachers to document student behaviors and their antecedents and consequences. Rarely do they invite teachers to personally reflect on their observations. Mentors can guide their beginning teachers in the reflection process by sharing that although reflection can be written narrative or oral dialogue, in order to be effective, it must include attitudes and feelings about the context and the behavior from both the student's and the teacher's perspectives. Mentors need to remind their beginning teachers that students choose behaviors because they meet a need; by identifying the need, the teacher may be able to move a student into a more desirable behavior that meets the same need.

Precautions and Possible Pitfalls

Mentors need to remind beginning teachers that even though they may reflect honestly negative feelings in their narratives, any written documents can be subpoenaed in a court of law. It is essential that narratives address the behavior—not the student—and be written in professional terms.

Source

Rao, S., Hoyer, L., Meehan, K., Young, L., & Guerrera, A. (2003). Using narrative logs: understanding students' challenging behaviors. *Teaching Exceptional Children, 35*(5), 22–30.

> *STRATEGY 51: Suggest that beginning teachers consider increasing the pace of instruction rather than reducing it when teaching students with special needs.*

What the Research Says

In his review of current practice and the research behind it, Heward (2003) cautions teachers who accept the idea that special educators should be patient and as a result lower their expectations for their students and ultimately slow the pace of instruction in an effort to demonstrate that patience. Heward (2003) argues that slowing the pace of instruction contributes not only to students' lagging attention but also to misbehavior and lack of skill acquisition. Heward (2003) cites the study of Ernsbarger (2002), in which students who were prompted using a variety of visual, auditory, and tactile prompts made greater reading skill gains than those who were required to respond independently. Wait time was decreased as reading skills increased until students were able to respond quickly and independently.

Application

Although there are many times when a good teacher will allow a student the needed wait time in order to facilitate a response, waiting may not always be the most effective practice. In applications where beginning teachers are requiring rapid responses from students with special needs, encourage beginning teachers to scaffold student responses by offering either visual or oral cues to facilitate skill acquisition. Learning math facts and sight words are two examples of curriculum that may be enhanced with a series of quick prompts. These cues can be faded over time as the response becomes more automatic for the student. Remind beginning teachers to pay close attention to student progress and level of interest. Using rapid pacing to heighten student interest will encourage the number of responses.

Precautions and Possible Pitfalls

 Be careful to monitor beginning teachers' pacing to ensure they are keeping students' attention focused. Check that they do not increase the pace to the extent that students become frustrated. Remind them not to slow the pace to the extent that students become distracted.

Sources

Ernsbarger, S. C. (2002). Simple, affordable and effective strategies for prompting reading behavior. *Reading and Writing Quarterly, 18*(3), 279–285.
Heward, W. L. (2003). Ten faulty notions about teaching and learning that hinder the effectiveness of special education. *Journal of Special Education, 36*(4), 186–206.

 STRATEGY 52: Suggest that beginning teachers facilitate their planning for students with special needs by using graphic organizers such as the Summary of Individualized Objectives (SIO)

What the Research Says

Although federal laws have moved more and more children with disabilities back into general education classrooms, the results have been somewhat mixed with regard to effective application of the IEP. Saint-Laurent (2001) identified that many general education teachers are not familiar with the contents of a student's IEP and so do not use it to help plan their instruction. In order to provide a vehicle to remedy this circumstance, she developed the Summary of Individualized Objectives (SIO). The SIO is a one-page graphic summary of all of the students who have special needs in a given inclusion classroom. The chart is prepared by the special education teacher and is divided into specific academic categories as appropriate (reading, writing, math, study skills, etc.). Under each topic the specific objectives each student is working on are listed.

The SIO is not just a tool used as a reference in the planning process but also serves as a communication device between the special education and general education teachers during the consultation process. As evaluation periods occur, the SIO can also be used to facilitate communication, making it an efficient process that can be updated as students meet their objectives.

The SIO is not the only graphic that can be used to facilitate this process. Teachers from a Maryland school district developed a similar approach linking state standards to student IEP objectives (Walsh, 2001). By using a chart to list the standards and then noting specific students whose IEP goals addressed those standards, teachers were able to quickly and effectively include those goals in their instructional planning.

Application

In order to facilitate lesson planning, mentors should sit down at the start of the year to help beginning teachers create a list of their students who have 504 plans or IEPs or who have specific accommodations or modifications. Notes on important details such as the student's learning style and goal area should be included. Depending on the subject area and grade level, beginning teachers might design a suitable chart that allows them to cross reference the essential standards they are required to teach and the goals their students have.

Mentors should be aware that some elementary teachers might find it more effective to create a chart that lists the students and the area of need by content area (Reading, Writing, Math, etc.). Other teachers, particularly those who teach single subjects, may find it more effective to create a chart that cross-references the state standards to the students' goal areas.

Whatever the method the beginning teacher chooses, it is important that he or she updates it as students achieve their goals. This chart can be used to track student progress and can be reported to parents at the regular reporting times in addition to the IEP meeting.

Sample SIO Charts

Elementary Level

Students	Reading	Writing	Math	Study Skills/ Behavior
Jeff	Identify main idea	Use correct spelling	Convert fractions into decimals	Complete tasks on time
Jessica	Read sight words	Produce sentences on topic	Use common denominators	Turn in all assignments
Fred	Increase reading fluency	Write a five sentence paragraph	Identify math terms in word problems	Use reference materials
Jorge	Use context clues	Put sentences in correct order	Use decimals when working money problems	Raise hand to participate in class

Secondary Level

Students	Goal Area	Accommodations/Modifications
Sabrina	Auditory memory, verbal production of complex sentences	Repeat directions, Books on tape
Geraldo	Track assignments and projects	Extended time on tests
Jon	Reading comprehension	Books on tape
Felicity	Reading and summarizing key elements	Extended time

Precautions and Possible Pitfalls

Although it is effective to keep a master list of students with special needs, mentors must emphasize to beginning teachers that this information must be kept confidential. Mentors should check that beginning teachers have avoided labeling the list "Special Ed" or something similar and they know to keep it away from the curious eyes of students and parents. Mentors may suggest to beginning teachers that if they use the chart to report on student progress, they should cover the parts that are not about that specific student before making any photocopies.

Sources

Saint-Laurent, L. (2001). The SIO: An instrument to facilitate inclusion. *Reading & Writing Quarterly, 17*(4), 349–356.

Walsh, J. M. (2001). Getting the "big picture" of IEP goals and state standards. *Teaching Exceptional Children, 33*(5), 18–27.

STRATEGY 53: Remind beginning teachers who refer students for special education assessments to consider all students, not just the students with obvious behavior issues.

What the Research Says

 In 2002, McCray and Garcia conducted a review of 27 years of research journals regarding issues of multicultural and bilingual special education. They identified concerns that have arisen in the research, including disproportionate representations, an inadequate supply of specially trained professionals, and a lack of culturally responsive services. They found gaps in the research—specifically from the people most affected by the research policy and practices. They call for improving special education services and delivery by emphasizing, " . . . authenticity, legitimization and multiplicity of voices" (McCray & Garcia, 2002). They note that few EL (English learner) teachers are trained in special education techniques and few special educators are trained in sheltered language instruction techniques. They also note that there is a significant lack of transition research for students of color. There is not just an overrepresentation of some groups but underrepresentation of other groups as well. Asian American and female students are under-represented in special education classes. They question if this is due to the difficulty in separating language issues from disability issues and comment that girls seem to exhibit fewer overt behaviors and so may go undetected.

Application

Although it is common for parents to refer their children for special education testing, the law requires districts to search and identify. Beginning teachers need to be cognizant of the issues affecting all students. For instance, it is vital that a student who speaks a second language be evaluated in that language for fluency prior to being placed in a classroom for special education service delivery. Likewise, students should not be excluded from receiving services based on language concerns.

As part of the observation and reflection process, mentors should encourage beginning teachers to carefully consider students who quietly fail. It can be a challenge to notice the student who sits in the back of the room barely meeting standards when the beginning teacher's attention is captured by the boisterous few who are excelling or creating behavior issues. Mentors should advise, when beginning teachers are grading student papers or entering grades in their grade-books, that they should take the time to reflect on each student who is hovering in that D–F range. Beginning teachers should consider the student's performance orally in comparison to his or her written assignments and consider test scores in comparison to project grades. Any discrepancy may be cause for further investigation. Mentors may wish to discuss what options exist at the particular site and how the beginning teacher can access them.

In addition, mentors may want to point out that students themselves often have insights and can articulate when a specific learning task is more challenging for them than for their peers. Although it is always a good idea to ask the student how he or she is doing in other classes or if he or she has noticed that a particular task is difficult, beginning teachers may feel that they are expected to be the experts and so may have difficulty approaching a student. Catching that frustration early may facilitate an early intervention.

Precautions and Possible Pitfalls

 Beginning teachers need to be aware of their own biases. Mentors may need to point out that we all have personal experiences that contribute to our perceptions and it is important to try to leave them out of the equation when referring students for additional help.

Source

McCray, A. D., & Garcia, S. B. (2002). The stories we must tell: Developing a research agenda for multicultural and bilingual education. *Qualitative Studies in Education, 15*(6), 599–613.

 STRATEGY 54: Encourage co-planning, co-teaching, and team efforts to support the needs of challenged students.

What the Research Says

Mentor teachers realize the benefits of collaborating with colleagues to problem solve and troubleshoot. In today's classrooms, the challenges new teachers face in trying to meet the educational, social, and emotional needs of diverse learners can be overwhelming. Teacher educators are increasingly realizing the benefits of teamwork. With school reform and restructuring and the "least restrictive environment" practice taking the spotlight, co-planning and co-teaching may provide powerful ways to address the demands of students with special needs (Hafernick, Messerschmitt, & Vandrick, 1997). Many schools are now using the model of co-teaching for their special needs populations. In this model the general education and special education teachers co-teach in the same classrooms.

In a 1999 study by Duchardt, Marlow, Inman, Christensen, and Reeves, the special education faculty of a university in Louisiana initiated collaborative opportunities with the general education faculty for co-planning and co-teaching. Teachers met once a week, over lunch, to discuss course content and lesson delivery. As an outgrowth of these meetings, meeting participants developed a co-planning and co-teaching model to assist other educators who wished to collaborate. A step-by-step design of this model follows.

Stage 1. Choose a trusted teacher with whom to collaborate. Obstacles can result when misunderstandings or miscommunications occur. The goal of collaboration is clear: success for special education students. The more this goal is discussed and used as a motivating factor, the more trust can be established and the greater the rapport that is generated.

Stage 2. Find pockets of time to plan. Carve out small blocks of time in the beginning to meet with other team members to discuss course content. Down the road, planning can occur on an as-needed basis, or even by phone or e-mail.

Stage 3. Brainstorm. After discussing course content, team members can brainstorm options for co-teaching the lesson. Brainstorming helps establish the expertise of each team member and permits planning to advance easily and without delay.

Stage 4. Prepare the actual lesson. The team members discuss, prepare, and develop a written guide for co-teaching the lesson. Consider having the lesson videotaped to assess and amend the lesson plan for future use.

Stage 5. Co-teach the lesson. The first time a lesson is co-taught, the two teachers must test the new instructional strategies. At this point, the preparation time will be obvious in its value. Until the lesson is taught, the teachers will have no idea if the first four strategies are working or if additional strategies for co-teaching will be needed. Once the lesson is done, the teachers can evaluate its success.

Stage 6. Support fellow team members. A necessary skill for the effective teacher to possess is the capability to be flexible and add to or emphasize key points throughout the lesson. Each team member needs to establish a comfortable and secure working relationship as well as trust in the intentions of the other team members.

Stage 7. Assess the lesson. After the lesson is presented, each team member can provide the presenting teacher with feedback. If the lesson was videotaped, team members can view the ways in which the lesson can be improved or polished. Having other trusted colleagues view the lesson might also provide valuable insights.

According to the study by Duchardt et al., co-planning and co-teaching arrangements can result in nine positive outcomes:

1. Collaboration and development of trust
2. Learning to be flexible and collegial
3. Finding pockets of time to co-plan
4. Learning through trial and error
5. Forming teaching and learning partnerships
6. Challenging ourselves and developing professionally

7. Solving problems as a team

8. Meeting the needs of diverse learners

9. Meeting the needs of teachers as problem solvers

Application

The African proverb "it takes a village to raise a child" can be adapted in education today to read, "It takes the whole school to educate a child." With the needs of special education students and other diverse learners, co-planning and co-teaching offer students (and teachers) opportunities for success. The collaboration between general education teachers, special education teachers, school counselors, speech therapists, and other school professionals can make a critical difference in helping students with special needs achieve. In one West Coast high school this model has been used extremely effectively. Taking a team approach has resulted in greater collaboration among all the staff members. The co-teaching model is so successful that other districts have come to observe and talk to participating teachers. General education teachers feel supported when dealing with their special needs students, and special education teachers can assist their students in succeeding in mainstream classes.

Precautions and Possible Pitfalls

Mentors know that while more and more schools are using a team approach when dealing with special needs students, caution should be taken. Team members must be committed to making this model work. Each member of the team provides expertise and insights critical to the success of students involved. Also, general education teachers sometimes aren't used to team teaching and may feel uncomfortable having other teachers in their classrooms. Mentors may need to help facilitate the progress of a new teacher who is team teaching. Team teaching should be just that. The special education teacher should not become an aide for the general education teacher but an integral part of the lesson. This is where planning is of critical importance.

Sources

Duchardt, B., Marlow, L., Inman, D., Christensen, P., & Reeves, M. (1999). Collaboration and co-teaching: General and special education faculty. *Clearing House, 72*(3) (Special Section: Culture and the Schools), 186–191.

Hafernick, J. J., Messerschmitt, D. S., & Vandrick, S. (1997). Collaborative research: Why and how? *Educational Researcher, 26*(9), 31–35.

STRATEGY 55: Recommend that beginning teachers use activity-based learning strategies when working with students with attention deficit/hyperactivity disorder (ADHD).

What the Research Says

In a recent study (Zentall, Hall, & Grskovic, 2001), researchers reported that the most effective instructional strategies for students with ADD/ADHD (attention deficit/hyperactivity disorder) were those that included personal attention, opportunities to be in leadership or helper roles, and the use of preferred activities as incentives. The least effective instructional strategies were those that took away or withheld activity.

Application

The frustrations of beginning teachers dealing with lesson planning, state testing schedules, classroom management, managing the paper load, and just trying to find enough hours in the day to accomplish it all can be overwhelming. Add to these responsibilities students with special needs (such as ADD/ADHD) and the new teacher may feel like he or she is navigating in choppy seas.

For a beginning teacher working with a special needs student, the first person to seek out for support can be a veteran special education teacher who has a thorough understanding of the student's IEP. Using a special education teacher to help plan activities and lessons can be a tremendous resource for the new teacher. The special education teacher can also provide helpful hints in dealing with discipline issues, preferential seating, and the importance of presenting clear, specific, and simple directions.

Stimulation through social interactions and activity-based lessons has been found to be effective with special needs students. Teachers should avoid lengthy doses of seat time and sedentary work. The use of hands-on and manipulative activities is also more effective with special needs students and may enable them to be successful. Providing the student with opportunities to move around the classroom can also be helpful. Allowing the student to run an errand, hand out papers, clean the board, or help out in the classroom can help reinforce appropriate behavior.

Because students with ADD/ADHD may experience greater difficulty in starting and organizing tasks, beginning teachers should consider breaking assignments down into smaller pieces while remembering to check for understanding at regular intervals.

Precautions and Possible Pitfalls

 Mentors need to remind new teachers that having a student with special needs in class can be challenging for any teacher. If the teacher is organized and has straightforward and concise classroom rules and procedures, with consequences clearly stated, the chances for student success increase. Beginning teachers need to be sensitive to students with special needs and not announce to the class that a certain student is allowed extra time on an assignment because of his or her disability. Most students with special needs don't want attention drawn to them. Mentors need to remind beginning teachers that any discussion of a student's disability should be done discreetly away from other students.

Source

Zentall, S. S., Hall, A. M., & Grskovic, J. A. (2001). Learning and motivational characteristics of boys with AD/HD and/or giftedness. *Exceptional Children, 67*(4), 419–519.

 STRATEGY 56: Recommend that beginning teachers use project-based learning strategies when working with at-risk students.

What the Research Says

Teachers of at-risk students tend to focus on basic skills, using traditional instructional methods such as whole-group lecture, repetitive drill-and-practice, and simple remedial exercises (Means, Chelmer, & Knapp, 1991). Students find these methods, when used almost exclusively, to be uninteresting, often resulting in reduced educational opportunities for the at-risk students. At-risk students are often not given the opportunities to learn using the advanced skills needed for problem solving and critical thinking.

Educational research indicates that project-based learning activities can help at-risk students learn and practice a variety of skills and improve their attitudes toward learning (Duttweiler, 1992; Means, 1994).

Application

Mentors know that to increase chances for at-risk students to be successful in class, while also providing skills needed for problem solving and critical thinking, teachers need to provide opportunities to participate in interesting and challenging project-based learning. The most beneficial project-based learning activities include six characteristics (Duttweiler, 1992; Means, 1994):

1. Opportunities to explore domains of interest

2. Active, interactive, and attractive instruction

3. Project orientation

4. Collaboration with peers

5. Opportunities to act as learner as well as designer

6. Opportunities to practice and develop fluency for advanced skills

By integrating technology with the curriculum, students have the chance to use technology to become more prepared for the job market as well as the demands of real life. The Web provides many sites with specific technology-based lessons prepared for students. Giving students choices, within project guidelines, allows for more student buy-in, practice in time management and organization, and a sense of ownership and empowerment. Teaming at-risk students in groups creates a greater chance for collaboration, self-esteem, and teamwork. Integrating project-based opportunities can provide students an effective instructional strategy for improving their chances of success.

Precautions and Potential Pitfalls

Beginning teachers should be careful to make sure that technology-based projects provide students the opportunities to browse diverse sources of information. The teacher should consult with knowledgeable colleagues and ask for their recommendations for projects. This way the projects can be age and ability appropriate and use academically relevant content. Mentors should caution new teachers not to rush to implement project-based activities without careful planning.

Sources

Duttweiler, P. C. (1992). Engaging at-risk students with technology. *Media and Methods, 29*(2), 6–8.

Means, B. (1994). Using technology to advance educational goals. In B. Means (Ed.), *Technology in educational reform: The reality behind the promise.* San Francisco: Jossey-Bass.

Means, B., Chelmer, C., & Knapp, M. S. (1991). *Teaching advanced skills to at-risk students: Views from research and practice.* San Francisco: Jossey-Bass.

8

Supporting New Teachers as They Develop Strategies for Embracing and Celebrating Diversity

I've come to the frightening conclusion that I'm the decisive element in the classroom . . . as a teacher, I possess tremendous power to make a child's life miserable or joyous . . . in all situations, it is my response that decides whether a crisis will be escalated or de-escalated and a child humanized or de-humanized.

Haim Ginnott

Theories and goals of education don't matter a whit if you do not consider your students to be human beings.

Lou Ann Walker

STRATEGY 57: *Help beginning teachers sensitize themselves to and embrace the diversity of today's classrooms.*

What the Research Says

 That today's schools are more diverse than ever is undeniable. According to the Federal Interagency Forum on Child and Family Statistics (1998), one in every three students currently attending primary or secondary schools today is of a racial or ethnic minority. Predictions are also that students of color will make up almost 50% of the U.S. school-age population by 2020 (Banks & Banks, 2001). With the large influx of immigrants in the past several decades, children of these immigrants make up approximately 20% of the children in the United States, providing a kaleidoscope of cultural and language differences in many classrooms (Dugger, 1998).

Cultural and language differences are only a part of the diversity in our schools. One in five children under the age of 18 currently lives below the poverty line. The traditional two-parent family is becoming the minority. Less than half of America's children currently live with both biological parents, with almost 60% of all students living in a single-parent household by the time they reach the age of 18 (Salend, 2001). All of this is occurring at a time when schools are working toward mainstreaming and the inclusion of nearly 11% of school-age children who are classified as disabled (U.S. Department of Education, 1995). Certainly the challenges that face today's classrooms have never been greater. Teacher preparation programs are including classes to help prepare future teachers for cross-cultural, inclusive instruction. Zeichner (1993) proposed that the key characteristics of these programs provide for the dynamics of prejudice and racism.

Application

Even in today's society some beginning teachers seem to be focusing on the differences and difficulties involved in multicultural education, rather than embracing these differences as being enriching, desirable, inevitable, natural, and welcome. Mentors should encourage beginning teachers to not only acknowledge the obvious diversity issues such as color and physical disability, but also be aware of the cultural diversity of students and families. Beginning teachers should be reminded when selecting curriculum that it is important to see if examples of diversity are represented. Mentors might pose the questions, Are the visual examples only of one race? Are the holidays represented in literature only those celebrated by one culture? Are the needs and emotions of people with disabilities presented?

Mentors may want to discuss instructional approaches with beginning teachers; for example, when having a discussion of families, it is important to stress that not all family units are alike. When sending a note home to parents, it is better to have it addressed to the "parent or guardian of" instead of "mother" or "father." Mentors might share a specific example to illustrate how innocent activities may be problematic for students. One teacher asked her students to describe their bedrooms and draw pictures of them. What this teacher didn't realize was that several students did not have their own bedrooms but shared the room with four or five other siblings. Disclosing this information to the class by reading their story and showing their drawings might have been embarrassing for these students.

By the same token, new teachers must be especially aware of district and state education codes with regard to celebrating religious holidays in the classroom. What about the student who doesn't celebrate Christian or Jewish holidays? Or what about the student who was a Jehovah's Witness and didn't celebrate birthdays (her own or others) and other "holidays" such as Valentine's Day? This student was sent outside while students exchanged valentines or celebrated a birthday with cupcakes. Rather than asking students to write a story about their favorite Christmas memory, the teacher might assign students to write about a favorite family tradition. One question a teacher should ask him- or herself is "Could this question, example, or assignment, make a student feel uncomfortable with regard to race, religion, ethnicity, or cultural background?"

Designing a richly diverse curriculum does not have to be difficult; it simply takes thought and consideration. The use of cooperative learning groups lends itself particularly well to teaching students with differing abilities in the same classroom. Students should be grouped with consideration to differences in gender, race, ethnicity, and ability. Using assignments and activities that incorporate the recognition of multiple intelligences is particularly necessary and effective in responding to student diversity.

Precautions and Possible Pitfalls

Mentors working with new teachers will frequently find it is beginning teachers who find themselves with the most diverse classroom. It is of the utmost importance that these teachers are prepared for cross-cultural, inclusive instruction. Mentors themselves should be trained or experienced in diversity training. Classes in teacher education programs must include information about the characteristics of prejudice and racism, provide successful examples of teaching ethnic- and language-minority students, and ingrain instruction that provides both social support for students and an intellectual challenge.

All teachers must be sensitive to issues involving economic status. Perhaps not every child in class can afford the cost of a field trip. For one high school that was considering putting ATM machines on campus, the realization of the ways this could further divide students into "haves" and "have-nots" caused administrators to rethink their decision. Federal law states that each student is entitled to a "free and appropriate public education." Students (and their parents) cannot be charged for lab fees, participation in extracurricular activities, field trips, etc. The outcome of the court cases is that students cannot be charged or be required to purchase instructional materials.

Beginning teachers should consult with experienced exemplary veteran teachers or school administrators before meeting with parents of immigrant students to determine if a translator might be needed or if there is any specific information about that student's family culture that might assist the teacher in having a successful meeting. Having a translator of the same sex as the parent may also be helpful. The more a teacher is sensitive to the richness of the diversity in his or her classroom, the more successful and equitable today's classrooms will become.

Sources

Banks, J. A., & Banks, C. A. M. (2001). *Multicultural education: Issues and perspectives* (4th ed.). New York: John Wiley & Sons.

Dugger, C. W. (1998, March 21). Among young of immigrants, outlook rises. *New York Times*, pp. A1, A11.

Federal Interagency Forum on Child and Family Statistics. (1998). *America's children: Key national indicators of well-being*. Washington, DC: U.S. Government Printing Office.

Salend, S. J. (2001). *Creating inclusive classrooms: Effective and reflective practices* (4th ed.). Upper Saddle River, NJ: Merrill.

U.S. Department of Education. (1995). *17th annual report to Congress on the implementation of IDEA*. Washington, DC: Author.

Zeichner, K. M. (1993). *Educating teachers for diversity*. East Lansing, MI: National Center for Research on Teacher Learning.

 STRATEGY 58: Foster site-specific awareness of diversity in the beginning teacher's school or district to support the development of culturally inclusive teaching practices.

What the Research Says

In 1990, Texas created its alternative certification program, and mentoring was a required element for all alternatively certified teachers. In 1991 it was mandated for all teachers. In order to gain an understanding of the most current status of teacher mentoring activities in Texas school districts, researchers conducted a statewide survey that was sent to district superintendents during the spring of 2000.

These data allowed the Southwest Educational Development Laboratory researchers to assess the scope, range of mentoring programs, mentoring activities, use of resources, and results. Data compiled represented 51% of all students in the state and 49% of all teachers. Responding districts reported student ethnic characteristics of 41% white, 41% Hispanic, 15% African American, and 3% other. Responding districts reported teacher ethnic characteristics of 72% white, 17% Hispanic, 10% African American, and 1% other. It is easy to see the demographic gap between the student and teacher populations within the racial and ethnic characteristics of responding schools.

These findings suggest that beginning teachers are indeed facing difficult challenges in classrooms and are "at-risk" of leaving their assignments when placed in highly diverse or low-achieving classrooms without the support of their more experienced colleagues. This Texas study pointed to a desire to give further attention to the needs of new teachers in diverse settings.

Application

Many respondents in this study prioritized the need to prepare teachers for the unique needs and learning styles of all students. However, there was little formal explicit support through mentoring in addressing the needs of diverse students by new teachers. The study found that the development of cultural awareness was discussed but not pursued through established induction elements that included mentoring. One school addressed the needs of diverse learners by screening during the hiring process for teachers who already demonstrated some level of awareness and competency in teaching in the diverse classroom.

Looking at the research demographic reveals a cultural mismatch with new teachers placed in cultural settings and situations that they had not experienced anywhere else in their lives. Across all districts it was found that first-year teachers were more likely to be assigned to highly diverse and low-achieving schools. In addition, attrition rates were notably higher for low-performing and diverse schools. These findings suggest that beginning teachers are being placed in assignments that present far more professional risks and challenges than in more suburban and less diverse schools. This study found no mentoring activities that focused on the support of new teachers in highly diverse settings.

Here is a list of selected topics that mentors may need to help their new teachers address:

- New teachers should expect a wide range of working conditions in low-achieving schools.
- Teachers in diverse settings need to explore and confront their own ethnic and cultural stereotypes.
- New teachers should learn to think beyond content regarding the needs of low-achieving or diverse urban settings.
- Should new minority teachers reflect their own ethnic and cultural identity to their students or project themselves as racially or ethnically neutral?
- How do teachers integrate multicultural connections into their curriculum?
- How do teachers embrace and utilize the cultural diversity of the school in the educational environment?

Often these are not topics those new to mentoring think about. Experienced mentors speak to guided and sheltered emersion in multicultural experiences as being the best teacher. Savvy mentors can learn to read a new teacher's readiness for an assignment and anticipate problems before they come up. Again, proactive is better than reactive. Ultimately, mentors want the new teacher to succeed for his or her students and embrace successfully the challenges of the diverse setting or low-achieving school.

Precautions and Possible Pitfalls

There are no real pitfalls in reflecting on these issues. However, the issues can be frustrating. There are no right answers that fill every individual need. For example, some native Spanish speakers claim that English immersion is the best way to treat English-language learners. Others are passionate advocates for various forms of bilingual education.

If a new teacher was once a language-minority student, he or she may be tempted to feel that the path personally taken toward success in school was the best one. These beliefs might be so strong they interfere with new information. The teacher's expectations for his or her students could be biased by his or her personal experiences. Sometimes these views are not supported by research, the school, or the district. The strategy that a teacher experienced may or may not be in touch with current thinking and educational research. The best that can be said is that new teachers have options to consider in how they perceive themselves, the identities they want to project as teachers, and how all of this fits into their own teaching and professional relationships.

Sources

Banks, J. A., & Banks, C. A. M. (2001). *Multicultural education: Issues and perspectives* (4th ed.). New York: John Wiley & Sons.

Dugger, C. W. (1998, March 21). Among young of immigrants, outlook rises. *New York Times*, pp. A1, A11.

Mutchler, S., Pan, D., Glover, R., & Shapley, K. (2000). *Mentoring beginning teachers: Lessons from the experience in Texas.* Austin, TX: Southwest Educational.

Development Laboratory. *Policy research report.* http://www.sedl.org/pubs/policy23.

Salend, S. J. (2001). *Creating inclusive classrooms: Effective and reflective practices* (4th ed.). Upper Saddle River, NJ: Merrill.

Zeichner, K. M. (1993). *Educating teachers for diversity.* East Lansing, MI: National Center for Research on Teacher Learning.

 STRATEGY 59: Be prepared to undo stereotypical beliefs and ideas that beginning teachers may bring from different social or cultural settings.

What the Research Says

High school films are a staple of the film industry, but in contrast to the suburban high school setting dealing with coming of age issues, the urban-high-school plot centers around gangs, drugs, violence, and similar topics according a review of the genre. In these urban high school films, classrooms are filled with socially troubled and low-achieving students and are dramatically transformed by the singular efforts of a teacher or principal, an outsider who is new to the school and often new to teaching entirely. All of this is accomplished to the surprise of administrative staff and other teachers, who never believed that these students had such potential.

Generally, the outsider succeeds where existing faculty, veteran professional teachers, and administrators have repeatedly failed. This research and related reviews and opinions argue that the urban-high-school genre of film reinforces the "culture of poverty" thesis and represents the stereotypical fantasies that suburban middle-class America has about life in urban high schools and the ease with which the problems in urban high schools could be rectified—if only the right type of person (a middle-class outsider) would apply the right methods (an unconventional pedagogy with a curriculum of middle-class norms and values). The teacher- or principal-hero represents middle-class hopes that the students in urban schools can be rescued from their troubled lives not through significant social change or school reform, but by the individual application of common sense, good behavior, a positive outlook, and better choices.

The basic idea here was to review the genre looking for stereotypical trends in how visible minorities are represented within the films. The researcher viewed each of these films and systematically took notes summarizing the major plot elements, the characterization, and the explicit and implicit lessons each film teaches. He took note of any variation in how urban, suburban, and private school films depict curriculum, pedagogy, the role of the teacher, the role of the administration, peer relations among students, extracurricular activities, the role of the family, the resources of the school, violence, drugs, and so on.

Application

In a quick Internet search for the "best" high school films at the Amazon.com site, the top 15 high school movies were cast by mostly white actors and were set in suburban schools. None of Amazon's top 15 movies took place in an urban setting. Most of the plots within these films dealt with coming of age issues. In contrast, within films from the urban school genre, coming of age plot descriptors were replaced with violence, gangs, drugs, and other similar genre terms.

In the urban school setting and plot a hero usually wins in spite of violence, drugs, and other stereotypical conditions in the urban school. The audience leaves feeling triumphant and optimistic about the potential for improvement in urban public schools if only the "right" people can show the students the way. However, by oversimplifying the many problems of urban public education and urban communities and turning inner-city students and public school teachers into caricatures of their respective social classes, these films do nothing but reflect middle-class anxiety about the problems of inner-city schools and the naïve hope that such problems need not a sustained political commitment from all members of society, but merely the individual moral conversion of the challenging students.

Assuming that many teachers and teacher candidates see these movies, how do these films affect their view of potential teaching positions in the urban setting? How are new teachers and teacher candidates going to negotiate social differences between teachers and their job setting, either real or imaginary? More importantly for the mentor, what view of the urban setting is coming with them?

How teachers view their students is a huge factor in how teachers develop their total educational environment. This includes developing expectations, standards, and aspirations. If the only view comes from Hollywood films, what are these expectations, standards, and aspirations going to look like?

As a mentor, the first job is to assess how new teachers view their students and the community they come from and, if needed, help them see the students and the location with new eyes.

In Levine's paper dealing with the identification of prospective multicultural educators, she proposed three factors that contributed to a high potential for successful inner-city teachers:

- "Prospective multicultural educators personally identify with educational inequality or social injustice. As a result, they have internalized a desire for change." As Haberman (1996) points out, the best educators for cultural diversity will not be those who conform to the traditional profile for new teachers.
- Prospective multicultural educators value critical pedagogy and a multicultural social reconstructionist education. Critical pedagogy and multicultural education are "mirror images" of each other. Grounded in principles of "personal liberation, critical democracy, and social equality," both approaches aim to change the unjust distribution of power in society. A more specific correspondence may be drawn between student-centered methods and multicultural education. When students are trained "in the cultural skills that improve their groups' traditions, such education prepares them to join the public discourse with confidence in their heritage."
- Prospective multicultural educators desire to learn more about educational inequality and its causes, including the social domination manifest in institutional racism and the practice of whiteness. White racialization and the effects of racial domination are a relatively recent yet expanding research focus within education.

What can mentors do to explore these ideas with new teachers? If these qualities are not present, what should mentors do? If they are, how can mentors use these qualities to the best advantage? There are too many variables here to develop absolute guidelines and rules. Separating stereotypical Hollywood ideas that new teachers might bring with them and replacing them with reality is a beginning. The mentoring skills that count the most are those geared to sustain realistic optimism and touch people with new possibilities.

Precautions and Possible Pitfalls

 Sociocultural, ethnic, and racial beliefs can be very personal and exist on a subconscious level. Dealing with these issues can be difficult for some. Some mentors might see a discussion of these issues as intrusive and too personal. They will have to be able to read their relationship and judge for themselves how and when to deal with these issues.

Sources

Bulman, R. C. (2002). Teachers in the 'hood': Hollywood's middle-class fantasy. *The Urban Review, 34*(3), 251–276.

Haberman, M. (1996). Selecting and preparing culturally competent teachers for urban schools. In Sikula, J. (Ed.) *Handbook of research on teacher education* (2nd ed., pp. 747–760). New York: Macmillan.

Levine-Rasky, C. (2001). Identifying the prospective multicultural educator: Three signposts, three portraits. *The Urban Review, 33*(4), 291–318.

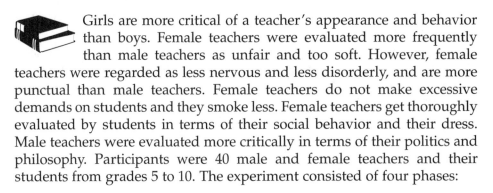

STRATEGY 60: Help beginning teachers see themselves through the eyes of their students.

What the Research Says

Girls are more critical of a teacher's appearance and behavior than boys. Female teachers were evaluated more frequently than male teachers as unfair and too soft. However, female teachers were regarded as less nervous and less disorderly, and are more punctual than male teachers. Female teachers do not make excessive demands on students and they smoke less. Female teachers get thoroughly evaluated by students in terms of their social behavior and their dress. Male teachers were evaluated more critically in terms of their politics and philosophy. Participants were 40 male and female teachers and their students from grades 5 to 10. The experiment consisted of four phases:

Phase 1: Questionnaire that asked students for their view of the characteristics of effective teachers

Phase 2: Observation of teachers' actions during lessons

Phase 3: Analyses of teachers' personalities

Phase 4: Procedures to improve or stabilize favorable teacher characteristics

The results showed that cheerfulness was the desirable characteristic that was named by students of all age groups. Most student views of the characteristics of effective teachers changed with the students' age. For example, being good at explaining facts was considered an effective characteristic by 34% of eighth graders, 41% of ninth graders, and 50% of tenth graders. The most frequent negative characteristics identified were being nervous, making excessive demands, being disorderly, being late, and smoking. Thirteen positive characteristics of effective teachers were identified:

1. Having good methodology
2. Identifying the aim of a lesson
3. Dividing tasks into parts
4. Supplying or demanding summaries of a lesson
5. Giving tasks with a high degree of difficulty
6. Getting students to think automatically
7. Not making intimidating comments
8. Involving students actively in learning
9. Not making discouraging comments when students make mistakes
10. Focusing on the essential points
11. Giving students individual help or making individual demands
12. Giving varied assessments
13. Evaluating a student's personality from a positive perspective

Application

 Teachers should be aware that gender characteristics affect how students view them. Female teachers are likely to find it harder to get students' respect than male teachers. Since cheerfulness was considered important by students of all ages, teachers could benefit from making a deliberate attempt to be more cheerful if they are not cheerful already. New teachers should look over the list from the research and use it as needed.

Precautions and Possible Pitfalls

Being polite, always speaking gently to the students, encouraging them, and so on are things that students expect from female teachers, but this alone does not work. A male teacher should not rely only on his professional knowledge. Although professional knowledge is important, there are other aspects of conducting a lesson that are important.

Source

Grassel, H. (1968). *Probleme und Ergebnisse von Untersuchungen der Lehrertätigkeit und Lehrerwirksamkeit* [Problems and results of investigations regarding teacher's activity and teacher's effectiveness]. Rostock, Germany: Studie des Wissenschaftsbereichs Pädagogische Psychologie der Universität Rostock.

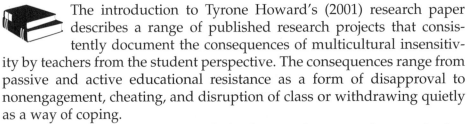

STRATEGY 61: Encourage beginning teachers to develop culturally responsive teaching strategies that align with students' ways of knowing, communicating, and being.

What the Research Says

The introduction to Tyrone Howard's (2001) research paper describes a range of published research projects that consistently document the consequences of multicultural insensitivity by teachers from the student perspective. The consequences range from passive and active educational resistance as a form of disapproval to nonengagement, cheating, and disruption of class or withdrawing quietly as a way of coping.

Howard's research examined the historical range of research that attempted to gauge the loudness of a multicultural student's voice in the educational equation all stakeholders share. Howard found that culturally relevant pedagogy recognized the cogent role that cultural socialization plays in how students receive, analyze, and interpret information. Culturally sensitive teaching and learning must go well beyond content modification. Modifying content does little to change how students perceive and respond to a noncaring environment.

Howard's study examined student perceptions and interpretations of instructional practices used by four elementary school teachers in four urban settings who were identified as culturally responsive teachers for African American students.

A total of 17 students were used in the study. Data were collected through observations and interviews with students. The purposes of student interviews focused on two areas. The first was to gain insight into viewpoints of ethnically diverse students that are rarely revealed in research about teaching and learning. The second was to balance the perceptions and interpretations of teaching practices between the student's viewpoint, the observer's viewpoint, and the teacher's intended goals and objectives.

Results indicate that culturally relevant teaching and learning should focus equally or more on how students are taught rather than what students are taught.

Application

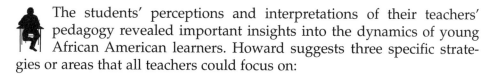 The students' perceptions and interpretations of their teachers' pedagogy revealed important insights into the dynamics of young African American learners. Howard suggests three specific strategies or areas that all teachers could focus on:

Caring: Explicit and implicit showing of sincere concern and care that teachers have for their students is vital. Positive reinforcement, expression of high expectations, and taking the time to find out about students' lives outside the classroom are vital to ethnic and cultural sensitivity. The commitment to both the academic and social development of students is the most important expression of concern and care.

Establishing community: The students in this study mentioned on repeated occasions their fondness for family- or community-like environments in their classrooms by encouraging kindred relationships in academic settings, the elimination of homogeneous ability groupings (both formal and informal), establishing appropriate democratic principles, and the promotion of interdependence.

Engaging classroom environments: Creating exciting and stimulating classroom environments is not a new idea, but this goes beyond the physical environment and focuses on the style of discourse. Connecting course content to the students' lives and modifying the style of discourse in ways that are more interactive, engaging, and entertaining for students are suggested.

Surprisingly, the study found that no students mentioned teacher race or ethnicity. The job for teachers is to acquire an understanding of the various cultural and learning characteristics their students bring to the classroom. Mentors can help here. New teachers who want to acquire an authentic understanding of the cultural aura students possess need, among other things, to abandon deficit-based stereotypes about the cognitive capacity, sociocultural backgrounds, and overall learning potential different ethnic groups bring to the classroom. There must be a willingness to make changes to pedagogy to align more with the students' way of knowing, communicating, and being. Far too often ethnic groups are asked or expected to leave their cultural identities at the door and conform to the teachers' way of thinking.

To make all this happen, teachers need to realize that this type of knowledge comes not only from books, but more importantly from parents, students, and community members. This may mean beginning teachers should immerse themselves in the day-to-day environment that the students experience. For new teachers, a strong will and courage may be their most needed asset.

Precautions and Possible Pitfalls

When developing effective teacher-student relationships, it is often difficult for new teachers to create clear, workable boundaries between the roles that all teachers have to play in dealing with students. Enabling questionable behavior in the quest for acceptance can create huge discipline and management problems. In the long run, setting reasonable and high standards for behavior, discourse, and pedagogy will establish a teacher's reputation as fair and culturally sensitive. By the time the second and third year of teaching roll around, a teacher's reputation will help alleviate misunderstandings about his or her role and teaching style and any expectations for his or her class before students enter the room. Finding a comfort zone in how a teacher deals with students takes time and is always considered work in progress. A teacher should look at establishing a three-year plan. Mentors can help here.

The teacher should try not to ignore the challenges students present or find quick-fix solutions, which usually means trying to adopt another teacher's system. Rather, the teacher should be reflective, examine personal core philosophies, and adjust them for more long-term solutions. A teacher should see good teaching more as a journey than a destination.

Source

Howard, T. C. (2001). Telling their side of the story: African-American students' perceptions of culturally relevant teaching. *Urban Review, 33*(2), 131–149.

 STRATEGY 62: Encourage beginning teachers to develop multicultural connections in all disciplines.

What the Research Says

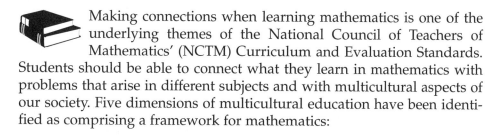 Making connections when learning mathematics is one of the underlying themes of the National Council of Teachers of Mathematics' (NCTM) Curriculum and Evaluation Standards. Students should be able to connect what they learn in mathematics with problems that arise in different subjects and with multicultural aspects of our society. Five dimensions of multicultural education have been identified as comprising a framework for mathematics:

1. *Integrate content* reflecting diversity when teaching key concepts.

2. *Construct knowledge* so students understand how people's points of view within a discipline influence the conclusions they reach.

3. *Reduce prejudice* so students develop positive attitudes toward different groups of people.

4. *Use instructional techniques* that will promote achievement from diverse groups of students.

5. *Modify the school culture* to ensure that people from diverse groups are empowered and have educational equality.

Application

All teachers should take into consideration that disciplines and content areas are not free of cultural influences, that some textbooks have racist biases, and that the history of any discipline should not just be viewed from a Eurocentric perspective (Pugh, 1990). Examples of how to apply the five multicultural dimensions to science include the following:

• *Integrate content* so that the history of the discipline's content knowledge comes from many cultures and ethnicities. For example, teach students about George Washington Carver, an African American who made major contributions that influence botany, agribusiness, and biotechnology.

• *Construct knowledge* so students see the universal nature of the components, concepts, and processes of the discipline and how other cultures and ethnic backgrounds might view them.

• *Reduce prejudice* by using teaching and learning that eliminate stereotypes. For example, balance the contributions of Caucasians with other ethnic backgrounds and cultures.

- *Use instructional techniques* that motivate students and demonstrate mutual respect for cultures. For example, group students from diverse cultures for cooperative learning activities, encourage all students to participate in extracurricular activities, and have high expectations for success from all students, regardless of diverse cultural backgrounds. Assign African American students to be tutors with white or Asian students as tutees.

- *Modify the school culture* by making special efforts to work with minority parents, especially those for whom English is not their native language, on improving their children's learning in science.

Precautions and Possible Pitfalls

 Teachers should make sure that multicultural aspects of lessons are not done in a patronizing manner. Also, they should try to be broad in their multicultural focus so that no particular cultural group (e.g., African American, Latino, Asian) feels it is being left out.

Sources

Banks, J. A. (1994). Transforming the mainstream curriculum. *Educational Leadership, 51*(8), 4–8.

Bishop, A. (1988). Mathematics education in its cultural context. *Educational Studies in Mathematics, 19,* 179–191.

Gallard, A. J. (1992). Creating a multicultural learning environment in science classrooms. *Research Matters to the Science Teacher, NARST News,* 34(14),1–9.

Mendez, P. (1989). *The black snowman.* New York: Scholastic.

Moses, R., Kamii, M., Swap, S., & Howard, J. (1989). The algebra project: Organizing in the spirit of Ella. *Harvard Educational Review, 59*(4), 423–443.

Pugh, S. (1990). Introducing multicultural science teaching to a secondary school. *Secondary Science Review, 71*(256), 131–135.

Strutchens, M. (1995). *Multicultural mathematics: A more inclusive mathematics.* ERIC Digest. Columbus, OH: Clearinghouse for Science, Mathematics and Environmental Education.

 STRATEGY 63: Remind beginning teachers that all cultures add value to schools and society and encourage them to reflect on and promote positive ethnic identities.

What the Research Says

This research focused on Latino teachers only, yet it makes it clear that the research has meaning for other ethnicities as well. The purpose of this preliminary study was to examine and explore ethnic identity and self-concept as they relate to preservice Latino bilingual teachers. Further, it began to answer questions that relate to relationships and school success within groups of language minority students. It proposed that a teacher with a strong and well-defined ethnic identity could have an impact on the academic success of students.

Multicultural contemporary classrooms now provoke issues such as the construction of racial and ethnic identities, gender roles, and socioeconomic status of students. Within this mix falls a teacher's sense of ethnic identity. Thus, teachers must be aware of the ways in which language, culture, and ethnicity mediate the social constructs of identity. How teachers perceive and interact with these constructs may affect the expectations teachers have for their students. In this study of Latino teachers and Latino students, the basic assumption made is that there is a correlation between how bilingual or ethnically diverse teachers perceive themselves and how they relate to their students. In comparing three ethnic groups' (white, black, and Chicano) self-conceptions, Hurstfield (1978) concluded that ethnic membership and status often determine an individual's self-description. Minority subjects were more likely than majority subjects to be conscious of racial or ethnic identity. The study cited past research that found connections between minority teachers sorting out and interpreting their cultural identity and those connections playing a critical role in their identity as educators. Carried further, they found connections between self-concept and teacher efficacy and empowerment.

The direct questions identified for this study were

- How do bilingual teachers identify themselves ethnically and what are their self-conceptualizations?
- Is there a within-group difference in how these Latino teachers identify themselves?

The subjects for this study were Latino students, mostly Mexican American, in a bilingual teacher education program at a major university in Texas. Ethnic identity as a psychological construct was established using an open-ended questionnaire.

First, analysis revealed that, for minorities, ethnic self-identification is an individual conceptualization. It is reflected in the heterogeneity found within groups, and ethnic labels are not always interchangeable. Second, it was important that individuals identify themselves too often as individuals who are stereotypically lumped together. Third, patterns within groups can be revealed. These three categories can be used to increase understanding of distinctiveness within minority groups. For example, some United States–born individuals identified themselves as Mexican even though they were not foreign born. Ethnic identity can often reflect how individuals recognize the sociopolitical context in which they live.

This limited study produced a variety of recommendations geared toward teacher education programs recognizing the need for minority teachers to struggle with questions regarding their teacher and ethnic identities. Above all, education programs need to address and value the cultural knowledge that minority teachers bring with them. They also need to recognize that their identity as educators will affect many areas of their interactions with students. Sometimes, this identity and cross-cultural literacy will mean more than their content knowledge in other areas of their teacher preparation.

Application

Like expectations held for teaching and learning environments, teacher education programs should value cultural knowledge and provide new teachers with the skills necessary to enhance the ethnic identities of their future students. New teachers placed in unfamiliar situations may need to be reminded of this. Because today's classrooms, more than ever, are cross-cultural environments, successful teaching is dependent on positive self-esteem. Ultimately, the way the school and its teachers respond to and support difference affects the degree of school success for many ethnic- and language-minority students.

The purpose of the study was to explore ethnic identity and self-concept as they related to preservice Latino teachers and to examine this relationship in regard to the school success of language-minority students. The researchers recommended that teacher education programs help minority preservice teachers with reflection on how they view themselves in the cultural or ethnic mix. Then they can decide how they see themselves as an ethnic person and how it all fits professionally in their teaching.

If a teacher's program didn't or doesn't provide this type of support, the teacher and mentor may be on their own in this exploration. A teacher should consider talking to trusted colleagues about the issues or seeking out additional academic research on the topic. There are no easy answers, as the individualistic nature of self-ethnic identification doesn't foster one-size-fits-all solutions and strategies.

Ultimately, some will see their calling as role models or advocates for their ethnic or cultural background and for language-minority or ethnic-minority students. Others will take the path of assimilation and not want their ethnic and cultural background to be an element in their teaching. Just becoming aware of the choices is a start.

Precautions and Possible Pitfalls

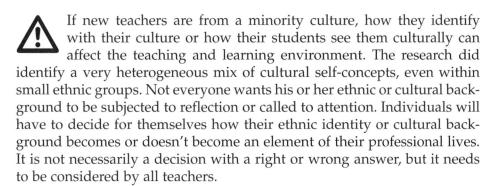

If new teachers are from a minority culture, how they identify with their culture or how their students see them culturally can affect the teaching and learning environment. The research did identify a very heterogeneous mix of cultural self-concepts, even within small ethnic groups. Not everyone wants his or her ethnic or cultural background to be subjected to reflection or called to attention. Individuals will have to decide for themselves how their ethnic identity or cultural background becomes or doesn't become an element of their professional lives. It is not necessarily a decision with a right or wrong answer, but it needs to be considered by all teachers.

Sources

Clark, E. R., & Flores, B. B. (2001). Who am I? The social construction of ethnic identity and the self-perceptions in Latino pre-service teachers. *Urban Review, 33*(2), 69–86.

Clark, E. R., Nystrom, N., & Perez, B. (1996). Language and culture: Critical components of multicultural teacher education. *Urban Review, 28*, 185–197.

Hurstfield, J. (1978). Internal colonialism: White, black, and chicano self-conceptions. *Ethnic and Racial Studies, 1*, 6–79.

STRATEGY 64: Encourage beginning teachers to explore and reflect on their own individual beliefs about privilege, bias, diversity, and multicultural education.

What the Research Says

Research on teacher expectations and student success suggests that a teacher's belief about students leads to differential expectations and treatment of students. Few qualitative studies aimed at understanding teacher beliefs about diversity and multicultural commitment have been done. This study utilized combined quantitative and qualitative methods to explore the attitudes, beliefs, and commitments of a predominantly Anglo-American population of preservice teachers enrolled in a diversity course. The results describe beginning attitudes, beliefs, and commitments to diversity; changes (or lack of change) in attitudes, beliefs, and commitments after participation in a diversity course; some theoretical underpinnings for understanding changes (or lack of change); and a framework for facilitating positive multicultural experiences.

The researchers found that encouraging multicultural understanding and commitment by provoking cognitive dissonance struck at the core of preservice teachers' belief structures. As a result, preservice teachers needed time and opportunity to gather information, think critically, reflect, converse, and assess and evaluate before making ideological decisions. Some were so strongly motivated by their existing beliefs that they chose not to explore some of the ideas presented in the course. Others assessed and rejected ideas, thus making their decisions following a period of exploration. Still others explored and accepted the new information either in whole or in part. These decisions were motivated by the need to be different, a willingness to be different, and an understanding of the kind of teachers they wanted to be. Preservice teachers shared that the authenticity of real experiences and hearing real stories of injustices done to real people made the difference in how they wanted to be as teachers.

Additional motivation to change occurred upon exploring alternative viewpoints and feeling empowered to make decisions for themselves following a realization that most of their beliefs and values were solely based on the values and beliefs of significant others in their lives.

The exploration of these values and priorities enables one to make choices in a deliberate manner, thus creating the opportunity for internalizing multicultural values and beliefs and increasing the likelihood of commitment and action.

Application

 Challenging new teachers to recognize the ethnocentricity and privilege associated with dominant-culture upbringing is an arduous process.

Currently there is little research that describes how new teachers attain, maintain, or adapt their belief structures in order to become multiculturally competent educators. Mentors can start with discussions about the new teachers' beliefs about diversity and increasing their commitment to a multicultural perspective. To begin, ask new teachers to reflect on (Middleton, 2002):

- Their beliefs about racism, classism, sexism, physical or emotional disabilities, and homophobia;
- The impact that their specific personal socialization in their cultural and socioeconomic setting influences their beliefs and behaviors; and
- The processes they must go through in uprooting misconceptions and focusing on the realities that exist in their new setting.

This can all be done in an authentic way. All mentors need to do is look at the new teacher's class roster to differentiate a range of diversity within the class. From there, mentors can begin to consider (Middleton, 2002):

- Approaching multicultural content as a positive and necessary component of the curriculum;
- Providing authentic cultural experiences;
- Assessing and addressing current levels of comfort and understanding of self and diverse others;
- Providing opportunities for self-reflection and dialog;
- Holding new teachers accountable for ethno-relative attitudes and behaviors; and
- Providing opportunities for instructors to dialogue about the strategies, triumphs, and pitfalls of teaching diversity.

The assessment and understanding of what new teachers currently believe about multicultural education and diverse others are critical steps in reducing prejudice, discrimination, and educational discrepancies (Middleton, 2002) occurring within educational settings.

From an institutional perspective these questions can be asked:

- Are new teachers being approached in a way that is nonthreatening and empowering rather than coercive?
- Are the instructors and experiences authentic (site specific) enough to reach the new teachers at both cognitive and affective levels?
- Are new teachers given enough time and opportunity to be made aware of and assess their current level of awareness, understanding, and ability in order to make informed choices regarding multicultural teaching practices?
- Is there a professional culture at the school of being supported, supporting each other, and supporting a multicultural curriculum?

Precautions and Possible Pitfalls

This whole dialog is based on a middle-class, Caucasian teacher moving into an urban environment. It is interesting to consider a new minority teacher moving into a Caucasian majority setting. Cross-cultural experiences can move many ways and directions. Bias and student profiling can occur from many perspectives. Unrealistic expectations can be fostered based on clothing style, peer group participation, and many other appearance factors. While this strategy is based on research on Anglo-American perspectives in a diversity course, there are many other ways teachers build bias into their interactions with their students. It pays to consider these also.

Source

Middleton, V. A. (2002). Increasing preservice teachers' diversity beliefs and commitment. *The Urban Review, 34*(4), 343–361.

 STRATEGY 65: *Remind beginning teachers to look beyond content to understand that English-language learners come with a variety of challenges and needs.*

What the Research Says

This research and reflection centers on the fact that one in four California students is an English-language learner. It also reflects on the fact that 90% of teachers in California are monolingual English speakers. This article examines how legislation and institutionalized practices affect teacher preparation in forcing teachers to accept roles emphasizing a standards-driven, technical, one-size-fits-all approach in addressing the very complex and diverse needs of English-language learners.

Focusing on California, the researcher (Balderrama, 2001) shows little faith in the ability of California's teacher certification programs to prepare teachers for meeting the needs of English-language learners or immigrant students. Critical reviews of credentialing practices in California range from the Cross-Cultural Language and Academic Development (CLAD) credential and California Basic Educational Skills Test (CBEST) to Reading in California (RICA) and the California Commission on Teacher Credentialing performance standards. She cites that standards or examinations don't provide any opportunity for examination of the role of the teacher in the socialization and schooling of youth. They tend to dance around the importance of culturally responsive teaching while de-emphasizing the more qualitative and affective aspects of teaching.

In apparent conflict are the standards-based assessment of good teaching and the more humanized standards most adults use to reflect on how they remember good teachers. In the end it is the humanity that is emphasized in reflection, not teaching methods, techniques, or implementing standards.

Concluding, the paper presents a context of teacher preparation with an emphasis on techniques and standards that tends not to prepare teachers in addressing the needs of an increasingly immigrant student population. The fear is that this lack of preparation will in turn not prepare the students academically.

Application

Teacher education programs are ideologically based, and new teachers need to understand the ideological underpinnings that tend to perpetuate social and economic subordination of marginalized populations. Mentors need to help new teachers find a balance in their role as a teacher from a technical perspective and sometimes, more important, a humanistic perspective.

When dealing with limited English proficiency students or English-language learners, new teachers will find that content and standards can be some of the least important things that they teach and learn in their lives. Balderamma (2001) states,

> In my attempts to raise the pedagogical consciousness of teachers, together we examine two elements of their teaching: 1) their students, within a historical context, and 2) the context of schooling and teaching. That is, students, particularly English-language learners, must be seen up close, not abstractly, so that understanding of their individual, academic and learning needs are [sic] humanized and thus fully understood.

Mentors should include a critical understanding of a sociocultural context in their instruction and also use it to help guide their practices.

This type of teaching doesn't call on new teachers to abandon all mandated guidelines, content standards, or expectations; it only asks them to find a larger and more relevant context within a larger picture of their students' lives.

Precautions and Possible Pitfalls

Beginning teachers need to be careful to "take the pulse" of their workplace. Colleagues may be under great pressure to raise test scores and student academic achievement. It would be a mistake for a teacher to ignore or neglect his or her responsibility to support school or department goals. However, a teacher can create a more humanistic educational environment in which the teacher and his or her students function. A teacher will be expected to be accountable, but that doesn't mean a teacher can't begin to explore a more humanistic approach to teaching and learning.

Sources

Balderrama, M. V. (2001). The (mis)preparation of teachers in the Proposition 227 era: Humanizing teacher roles and their practice. *Urban Review, 33*(3), 255–267.

Valdez, E. O. (2001). Winning the battle, losing the war: Bilingual teachers and post-Proposition 227. *Urban Review, 33*(3), 237–253.

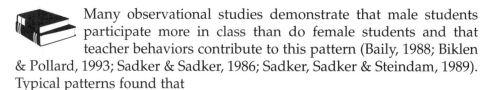

STRATEGY 66: Assist beginning teachers in recognizing and eliminating signs of subtle gender bias in the classroom

What the Research Says

Many observational studies demonstrate that male students participate more in class than do female students and that teacher behaviors contribute to this pattern (Baily, 1988; Biklen & Pollard, 1993; Sadker & Sadker, 1986; Sadker, Sadker & Steindam, 1989). Typical patterns found that

- Male students receive more attention and more specific feedback from teachers.
- Males are more likely to receive praise for the intellectual content of their answers.
- Teachers rarely wait more than five seconds for a response to questions and rarely call on nonvolunteers. This type of discourse favors aggressive male students.
- Many teachers are unaware of their own discriminatory behaviors until someone calls them to their attention.
- Gender equity is rarely a component of teacher education programs.
- Teachers have a misconception that they are not responsible for bias in the classroom and the students are. If teachers believe that students, not teachers, are to blame for gender bias, it will continue.
- Prospective teachers' beliefs may interfere with current concepts and ideas in gender-bias components of teacher education.

In this study 48 preservice teachers (21 male, 27 female) were involved in trying to answer the following questions:

1. How do preservice teachers' perceptions of gender interactions compare with actual gender interaction data?

2. Do prospective teachers become aware of the limits of their own perceptions in detecting inequities in classroom interaction?

3. What strategies do preservice teachers propose to ensure equity?

4. Do preservice teachers report changing any beliefs about subtle gender bias?

These preservice teachers were all enrolled in sections of an educational psychology class. Gender interaction patterns were recorded and researched using a variety of techniques both in their classes and during outside field experience. Some of the highlights of their results included the following:

- Seventy-three percent said they would promote equity and make a conscious effort to ensure equity in seating, lab work, cooperative groups, and athletic activities and ensure equity in curriculum content and language use.
- Twenty-four percent said they would collect data to become aware of or to monitor gender bias (videotape, outside observers).
- Twenty-one percent said they would become more aware of seating arrangements and pairing of males and females.
- Eighteen percent said they would balance guest speakers and gender bias in curriculum.
- Several planned to use inclusive language to switch gender roles for demonstrations, clean-up, and so on.
- Thirty-five percent of the students reported changes of conformations of their beliefs about gender equity.

In discussions, it was felt that interventions of this sort in teacher education programs increased awareness of gender bias. The majority of students discussed the need to collect data and monitor classroom interaction in order to ensure equity in their future classrooms. The answer to question four seemed to be beyond the scope of the study.

Application

 There are two categories of action that beginning teachers can take from this research.

1. Believe that gender bias exists and just as in preparing other components of pedagogy keep gender bias as a highly considered element. They should view existing research on the subject and adjust teaching style where it is needed.

2. Informal action research can alert a teacher to subtle biases he or she may not be aware of. Mentors can videotape a teacher's interactions or

document an observation of the teacher's lesson. Mentors should include the number of boys called on versus girls, discrepancies in wait time by gender, or asking for helpers who are all of the same gender. At the post-observation meeting the mentor can address areas of concern that relate to gender and together decide on appropriate changes to instructional strategies and classroom discourse.

Most of the students in the study believe that if they had not experienced gender bias it was because they were not really aware of it. Once they became aware of the fine details of gender bias in the classroom, the project showed them that their perception might not fit reality.

Precautions and Possible Pitfalls

Boys and girls have acquired their behaviors and roles over time. They need to be taught how to recognize gender bias in their own lives. There are many students who are so comfortable in their roles that they would resist changing. Beginning teachers should consider keeping their equity goals as part of a hidden or subtle curriculum. Students acquired their roles over a long time and from many places, and teachers should keep their expectations reasonable. The teacher may not see the desired changes in the short time he or she works with the students.

Sources

Baily, G. D. (1988). Identifying sex equitable interaction patterns in classroom supervision. *NASSP Bulletin, 72*, 95–98.

Biklen, S. K., & Pollard, D. (1993). *Gender and education. Ninety-second yearbook of the National Society for the Study of Education (part 1).* Chicago: University of Chicago Press.

Lundeberg, M. A. (1997). You guys are overreacting: Teaching prospective teachers about subtle gender bias. *Journal of Teacher Education, 48*(1), 55.

Sadker, M., & Sadker, D. (1986). *Failing at fairness: How America's schools cheat girls.* New York: Scribner.

Sadker, M., Sadker, D., & Steindam, S. (1989). Gender equity and educational reform. *Educational Leadership, 46*(6), 44–47.

 STRATEGY 67: Remind beginning teachers that students (especially male students) sometimes treat female teachers differently than male teachers.

What the Research Says

The researcher interviewed 16 women from three teacher education programs in New England to learn about their experiences as female student teachers and acquire insight into the gender issues in female student teachers' lives. More than half the women interviewed spoke of being demeaned and objectified. One of the most evident gender issues coming from the study was male high school students' harassment of female student teachers. They told stories of how the cultural habit of viewing women as sex objects affected the environment in which they began teaching.

An in-depth interviewing technique was used to gather information related to specific incidents and how these related to their lives and what it was like as a woman to student teach. The predominant complaint centered on how male students feel entitled to exert power in a school context and demean and dehumanize female student teachers through objectification. Other male students are often mute or provide open support to these behaviors. Their behaviors are described as a power struggle between genders. Male students, who, especially in secondary schools, are relegated to lower power relationships, grab control by transforming the recognized authority in the room to a powerless object of their discourse. Language becomes their weapon.

Application

Mentor teachers and beginning teachers must develop ways to first become aware of gender issues embedded in management, curricular, and discipline issues and then become more cognizant of the gender factors within their context. Many can arise from deeply rooted sexist attitudes both within the teachers themselves and within their students.

There are culture-driven gender issues that female teachers must confront in their own thinking. The study pointed to a critical juncture during the middle school years in which girls either learn to be honest about what they see around them and know or deny what they see and know. The researchers found that when the girls confront individuals or institutions in their lives, they risk losing relationships with parents, teachers, and friends. If they remain silent, they are more likely to maintain peaceful relationships with these people. Most girls choose silence. When these women make the transition from student to teacher, from dependence to independence, from passive to active initiator, they need a reservoir of support to draw from. There is a residue from growing up female in the U.S. culture, and this residue can show up again at this vulnerable time of learning to teach.

Another problem lies within potential supporting collaborators. Not everyone in the support context may possess enough insight, experience, or empathy to help. Not everyone has the insight to recognize potential gender issues.

Precautions and Possible Pitfalls

 Mentors should remind new teachers not to overreact and make every sexist remark, look, or comment their own problem. New teachers should pick their battles carefully and tread lightly, as some of these entrenched attitudes are invisible to the students themselves. In all likelihood each incident will need to be treated differently and a different strategy will be needed. Mentors can assist new teachers with appropriate strategies based on their observations.

Source

Miller, J. H. (1997). Gender issues embedded in the experience of student teaching: Being treated like a sex object. *Journal of Teacher Education, 48*(1), 19–28.

 STRATEGY 68: Encourage beginning teachers to be sensitive to issues affecting gay and lesbian youth.

What the Research Says

Several research studies suggest that approximately 1 in 10 of the students served by public schools will develop gay and lesbian identities before graduation (Cook, 1991; Gonsiorek, 1988). Sexual orientation, however, appears to be established prior to adolescence, perhaps from conception, and is not subject to change (Gonsiorek, 1988; Savin-Williams, 1990).

The social stigma surrounding homosexuality discourages many gay and lesbian teens from discussing the confusion and turmoil they may feel about their emerging identities (Friend, 1993). Add to this sense of confusion the isolation they may feel, and it should not come as a surprise that gay and lesbian youth are "two to six times more likely" than heterosexual teens to attempt suicide. While gay and lesbian teens account for 30% of all completed suicides among adolescents, they comprise only 10% of the teen population (Cook, 1991).

Application

Mentors need to be aware that almost every district has specific nondiscrimination policies regarding both employees and students. With recent court decisions regarding sexual harassment, beginning teachers must be knowledgeable of these policies and take responsibility for their being upheld.

Gay and lesbian youth face many of the same changes with regard to social, biological, and cognitive development as their heterosexual counterparts. However, the misconceptions and stigmas, combined with the homophobic cultural climate of our society, often add to the stress and turmoil that many of our gay and lesbian youth struggle with on a daily basis.

Adolescence is a difficult time at best, and these years can be hell on earth for students struggling with issues relating to their sexual orientation. Students can be very cruel to each other, and this seems to be heightened during adolescence. The physical and emotional safety of every student in class should be paramount. Teachers of middle and high school students can do a lot to provide a safe and harassment-free environment. Beginning teachers may be reluctant to address such controversial issues in their classrooms, but it is essential that they do so. Not allowing derogatory words or comments in class is a start. If a teacher does not address these negative comments, the gay or lesbian student can further feel alienated and alone. Silence from the teacher is interpreted many times as agreement with what is being said. Because homosexuality appears to be one of the last bastions of "acceptable" discrimination, our gay and lesbian youth may feel more isolated and withdrawn than our heterosexual students. These perceptions of inferiority can lead to poor self-esteem, substance abuse, sexual promiscuity with the opposite sex (to conceal their true feelings), and possibly suicide. Teachers would not tolerate students calling each other by racial, ethnic, or religious slurs; therefore we must not tolerate comments of a negative nature to our gay and lesbian students either.

It is up to each and every teacher to provide a safe, nurturing, and respectful environment for every student.

Precautions and Possible Pitfalls

Just because a beginning teacher doesn't have a student (or students) coming out to him or her doesn't mean that teacher doesn't have any gay or lesbian students in the classroom. Given many research studies that estimate 1 in 10 persons are homosexual, it stands to reason that in a class of 30 students a teacher might have three who are struggling with sexual orientation issues. New teachers shouldn't assume that if no one is coming forward to complain about harassment or name calling, then the problem doesn't exist. This type of sexual harassment is the most common form found on middle and high school campuses today.

Students may pose questions to the teacher about homosexuality (Is it OK? Why are some people heterosexual and some people homosexual? etc.). It is not advisable to get into a discussion of right and wrong, OK or not OK. However, telling students that *every* person is entitled to respect, acknowledgement, and acceptance is not only OK; it is the right thing to do.

Sources

Cook, A. T. (1991). *Who is killing whom?* Issue Paper 1. (Available from Respect All Youth Project, Federation of Parents and Friends of Lesbians and Gays, P.O. Box 27605, Washington, DC 20038).

Friend, R. A. (1993). Choices, not closets: Heterosexism and homophobia in schools. In L. Weis & M. Fine (Eds.), *Beyond silenced voices: Class, race, and gender in United States schools* (pp. 209–235). Albany: State University of New York.

Gonsiorek, J. C. (1988). Mental health issues of gay and lesbian adolescents. *Journal of Adolescent Health Care*, 114–122.

Savin-Williams, R. C. (1990). Gay and lesbian adolescents. *Marriage and Family Review, 14,* 197–216.

9

Supporting New Teachers as They Develop Strategies for Working With New Technologies

Sixty years ago I knew everything; now I know nothing; education is a progressive discovery of our own ignorance.

Will Durant

 STRATEGY 69: Remind beginning teachers not to let technology overwhelm subject matter.

What the Research Says

A traditional undergraduate physics course on math methods was redesigned to incorporate the use of a computerized algebra program throughout all aspects of the course. The goal of this redesign was to expose beginning students to professional tools currently used by mathematicians and physicists. At the same time, a new multimedia physics class sought to integrate math and physics content with other multimedia forms. These two classes served as research laboratories to begin a qualitative case study to first describe the course and then develop an understanding of the effect technology had on instruction and learning in the courses. It was found that the instructors of both courses made rather substantial changes in their courses the second time through based on their early experience.

The research provided an overview of the issues as follows:

• Students resisted the additional process orientation of adding technology as another layer of course requirements. Computers add another layer of process skills to learn.

• Teachers needed to be better prepared and have their own technological act together.

• The advanced workload preparing for such courses is enormous and goes unnoticed by the students. To the students, book content represents the curriculum: A reduced use of books leads to a student perception of a reduction in structure.

• There needs to be a means for demonstrating the technology and a backup plan in case of problems.

• Clear procedures needed to be developed for students to follow when they encountered problems.

• Whenever students seemed to have strong learning preferences and styles, their expectations about how they "ought to be taught" conflicted with the design of the courses. Expectations need to be described explicitly and explained for possible conflicting expectations. Problematic conflicts in how and why instruction is implemented need to be resolved.

• Instructors somewhat underestimated the basic instruction needed. Teachers were challenged to provide guidance and examples without providing "simple" templates that structure the students' homework with little imagination or editing. Technology used as a professional tool required in-class instruction that modeled real problem-solving modes.

Overall, the research suggested that the necessary transition from traditional instruction to tool-based instruction is dramatic and fraught with difficulty for teachers and students. The researchers found their data far less positive or encouraging than they would have liked. As experienced teachers, as technology users, and as scientists foreseeing drastic changes in the kinds of intellectual skills that students are likely to bring to the professional world, they saw a long developmental road ahead.

Application

When movable type was invented and the first books printed, none of the formatting, running heads, tables of content, page numbers, indexes, and so on were included. The "technology" of the book is standardized today. When new teachers teach a course from a book, most of the time all involved know what to expect.

Calculators, seen as routine today, required a good deal of time to filter through instructional practices and find a niche. Most teachers today have no problem finding a context in their courses for calculators. There are no such standards yet for the World Wide Web.

As new technology continues to filter into the classroom, beginning teachers need to address the concerns listed in the research and accept a rather steep learning curve for implementing technology for themselves and their students. The researchers found a remarkable similarity in problems and pitfalls between these two independent classes using very different technologies. Real-world professional tools impose a rather drastic transition for all stakeholders. New teachers need to become as informed as they can about the technology but also be aware of the potential transitional pitfalls they will need to address as a professional educator.

Precautions and Possible Pitfalls

Mentors need to remind beginning teachers to not underestimate the amount of work involved in making technological transitions both for themselves and for their students. Frustrated students can sabotage their best efforts by not authentically engaging in the new type of instruction. Students who would do well in traditional classes need nurturing and assurance when the rules change.

Source

Runge, A., Spiegel, A., Pytlik, L., Dunbar, S., Fuller, R., Sowell, G., & Brooks, D. (1999). Hands-on computer use in science classrooms: The skeptics are still waiting. *Journal of Science Education and Technology, 8*(1), 33–44.

STRATEGY 70: *Encourage beginning teachers to use the Internet as a classroom.*

What the Research Says

"Kids as Global Scientists" (KGS), characterized as a telecommunication program, is an interactive, integrated, inquiry-based science curriculum project that has been developed by meteorologists and teachers from the University of Michigan and is sponsored by the National Science Foundation. It resides on the Internet, which makes it accessible to large numbers of teachers and students. Its current Internet project engages over 200 schools in interactive investigations. Professional weather experts interact with students, answering their questions. The total length of a unit runs 6 to 8 weeks.

The investigation and interaction is facilitated by the use of specialized interactive software that is designed specifically for the project. The software provides all textbook content and, in addition, connects students to the Internet, simulations, and current imagery collections of weather data and allows them to download data. In one project the program suggests a final project of building a hurricane-safe house and simulating the force of the hurricane by using a leaf blower.

The program provides teacher's guides, software, and all other material needed to empower the project. The program develops thematic units within the earth science discipline of atmospheric science and meteorology.

Research centered on the assessment and evaluation of one class participating in one unit or program. Six sixth-grade students representing three motivational levels were selected for intensive study to help illustrate how different students view learning science and the use of technology both before and after a technology-rich program. Pre- and post-assessment scores were analyzed for the entire class, and the six students' comments from individual interviews provided one example of evidence from each motivational level.

Overall, results indicated significant gains in content knowledge and a high level of motivation with the project. Students find the use of the Internet and telecollaborative environments engaging and motivating.

Application

Use of the Internet as a classroom is an emerging application of the technology. Mentors know that in addition to the KGS program, there are other such opportunities to engage students in similar programs. Distant learning (type the term in a search engine and you will find a large numbers of sites) is available as an alternative to site-dependent learning. Many colleges and universities and a few high schools now offer participation in digital classrooms. Electronic advance placement classes are now offered as alternatives for schools without the ability to provide such programs.

As an inquiry-based science experience, KGS offers an authentic, guided, safe experience that is not only content but also process rich. The use of technological tools provides a motivating vehicle to learn. Not all science works this easily in real life. However, for a taste of real science, this serves the purpose. The Internet educational market is growing. The KGS project is a packaged user-friendly project.

NoodleTools, at www.noodletools.com, is a free suite of interactive tools designed to aid students and professionals with their online research. From selecting a search engine and finding some relevant sources and then citing those sources in MLA style, NoodleTools makes online research easier.

There are a number of Internet sites that act as repositories of data. Climate and weather data are easily available, and the GenBank provides almost unlimited genomic and molecular science data. Imaginative, creative, and motivated teachers can develop their own inquiry-based opportunities. Many of these sites offer free data that can be used to answer student questions. The opportunities are open-ended in nature and can be as complex or as simple as the instructor desires. There are even digital libraries that offer access to periodicals and other sources of information. Some access is limited to subscribers and some sites must be accessed at a college or university that subscribes to the service.

There are too many sites to identify here. At the time of writing this strategy, typing the term *interactive lessons* in a search engine produced over 5,000 hits. Not all these sites are useful, but it does give new teachers the idea there is a lot out there.

Precautions and Possible Pitfalls

Although the technology provides an exciting and often motivating alternative to conventional hands-on experiences, the evaluation and preparation time remains the same. It is essential that new teachers take time to survey and evaluate the potential that specific Internet sites offer. Technology has its quirks and breakdowns, and access may not be available on demand or on the class's schedule; mentors may need to remind new teachers to include alternatives in their lesson planning just in case.

Source

Mistler-Jackson, M., & Songer, N. (2000). Student motivation and Internet technology: Are students empowered to learn science? *Journal of Research in Science Teaching, 37*(5), 459–479.

STRATEGY 71: Remind beginning teachers that some students know computer technology better than others, and some may know it better than the teacher does.

What the Research Says

The effectiveness of instructional methods when teaching students to use a computer application depends upon students' prior knowledge of the material you are teaching. A study was conducted with students learning to use a database program. Students in one condition were given worked-out examples of how to use the program; students in the other condition explored use of the program in a discovery fashion. Classroom instruction in the computer application preceded students' participation in the two conditions. The results showed that worked-out examples were much more efficient with students who had limited prior knowledge, while this benefit evaporated for students with more prior knowledge. Students who had prior knowledge were able to activate and use it during discovery learning, thereby enhancing their efficiency.

Application

Consider strategies to help new teachers organize their students when there is a technology component to be learned within classroom instruction. Teachers may want to group students homogeneously for learning to use computer applications based on their prior knowledge, so that more-experienced students use discovery learning, while less-experienced students start with worked-out examples.

Teachers could also group students heterogeneously, having more-experienced students work with less-experienced students during discovery learning, so that the more-experienced students can teach or guide the less-experienced students in their discovery learning.

Precautions and Possible Pitfalls

If a new teacher decides to group students homogeneously, he or she shouldn't keep students working permanently using worked-out examples. Once they have experience in the content area, the teacher should encourage them to apply what they have learned through discovery learning.

Source

Tuovinen, J. E., & Sweller, J. (1999). A comparison of cognitive load associated with discovery learning and worked examples. *Journal of Educational Psychology, 91*(2), 334–341.

STRATEGY 72: Familiarize beginning teachers with the International Society for Technology in Education (ISTE) and its standards for student learning in technology.

What the Research Says

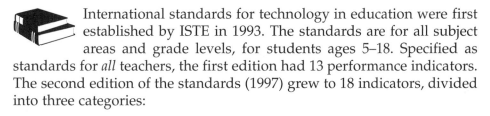

International standards for technology in education were first established by ISTE in 1993. The standards are for all subject areas and grade levels, for students ages 5–18. Specified as standards for *all* teachers, the first edition had 13 performance indicators. The second edition of the standards (1997) grew to 18 indicators, divided into three categories:

1. Basic computer/technology operations and concepts

2. Personal and professional use of technology

3. Application of technology to instruction

The third edition of the standards, ISTE National Educational Technology Standards for Teachers, consists of 23 performance indicators that are grouped into six categories:

1. Technology operations and concepts

2. Planning and designing learning environments and experiences

3. Teaching, learning, and curriculum

4. Assessment and evaluation

5. Productivity and professional practices

6. Social, ethical, legal, and human issues

Technology is not only here to stay, its influence is exploding exponentially in education and all other aspects of life. Teachers need to integrate it into their instruction now or their students will be left behind in the future.

The RAC (research, analysis, and communication) model is an instructional framework for integrating technology into the curriculum through lesson planning and assessment across subjects and grade levels. Research suggests that teachers identified the following benefits of RAC lessons:

- It allows more student-centered learning.
- Students engage in more critical thinking.
- Material can be integrated across subject areas.
- It is easily incorporated into performance-based classrooms.
- Students are required to apply important skills in a meaningful context.
- It provides opportunities to evaluate students' work.

Application

To plan the use of technology to meet the national standards for both teachers and students, new teachers can visit the ISTE Web site (www.iste.org) and download or view the standards. The Web site also has numerous instructional resources to help teachers integrate technology into their instruction in virtually all grades and subjects. Resources include a database of lessons in which a teacher can search for lesson plans that integrate technology into science teaching, specifying the particular topic and grade level. The site also contains resources that have been developed for multidisciplinary units and allows teachers to enter their own lesson plans.

According to the ISTE Web site, the "Multidisciplinary Unit Resources" section includes resource units designed to provide powerful themes around which multidisciplinary learning activities can be built. Each unit addresses the theme with a variety of activities, related technology, and thematically relevant information, tools, and resources. Each activity is designed to address content standards from two or more subject areas while also addressing the National Educational Technology Standards (NETS) for students' performance indicators. Units for each grade range provide developmentally appropriate themes, tools, and resources from which teachers can choose when developing specific learning experiences.

Implementing the RAC model involves the following three phases:

1. **Research.** Students gather information from various resources. For example, they go to various Internet sites to acquire information about specific concepts within the curriculum.

2. **Analysis.** Data analysis depends upon the results of the research. Students must think critically and use the information they gathered. For example, like paper resources, students have to gauge the validity of the

information, whether it is the most current, biased, or complete enough for their use.

 * 3. **Communication.** Students prepare products to share their results. For example, students can communicate the new information to a wider audience for critical review and critique.

Precautions and Possible Pitfalls

Teachers, especially new teachers, should not expect themselves or their students to meet all of the 23 performance indicator standards the first or second time around. Teachers and their students may need more time and experience to assimilate new information and develop new skills. Teachers can use the standards as longer-term goals and establish performance criteria for assessment purposes. The topic could make a good department goal.

Source

Bowens, E. M. (2000). Meeting standards with technology. *Learning and Leading With Technology: Serving Teachers in the Classroom, 27*(8), 6–9, 17. Retrieved from www.iste.org

STRATEGY 73: Insist that beginning teachers develop Internet-based literacy.

What the Research Says

Bos (2000) conducted research to examine the Internet as a source of valid information for science students. The World Wide Web is an exciting and challenging information resource now available to many teachers and students. It is so convenient for students it can become their primary source of information while conducting research for their assignments and projects. The Internet is challenging because of the diverse and often uneven nature of the information presented. This presents both students and teachers with the need to develop new skills of critical analysis and evaluation. Critical evaluation skills have always been an important part of media literacy for students in the context of a science class. Bos's study focused on two aspects of critical evaluation: summarization of science content and evaluation of credibility.

Participants in Bos's study were students in two 11th-grade science sections at an alternative high school in a medium-sized midwestern college town. The class involved in these studies was in the third year of a

"Foundations of Science" sequence, an integrated science curriculum that follows the principles of a project-based approach. It also has a heavy technology component. Forty-four students (27 females and 17 males) took part in the project. The study centered on answering three questions:

1. Can students summarize scientific resources that they find on the Web?

2. Can students identify and evaluate evidence in the scientific resources that they find on the Web?

3. Can students identify the source and potential biases (points of view) of the scientific resources that they find on the Web?

The project produced 63 student Web reviews published by the students. Content analyses showed that student summaries were usually accurate. However, students had problems assessing how comprehensive and detailed sites were. When asked to evaluate credibility, students struggled to identify scientific evidence cited or presented supporting Web site claims. This was a problem because many Web sites do not present evidence as it might be found in a scientific journal format. Students could determine the publishing source but were challenged in identifying potential biases with Web publishers.

The findings of Bos's study can provide teachers with a solid grounding for further development of media literacy activities. Technical and pedagogical scaffolding based on site-specific goals and demands facilitates students' acquiring or reinforcing critical evaluation skills.

Application

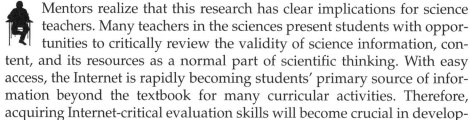 Mentors realize that this research has clear implications for science teachers. Many teachers in the sciences present students with opportunities to critically review the validity of science information, content, and its resources as a normal part of scientific thinking. With easy access, the Internet is rapidly becoming students' primary source of information beyond the textbook for many curricular activities. Therefore, acquiring Internet-critical evaluation skills will become crucial in developing overall media literacy.

There are many ways to embed critical evaluation into projects or as a separate independent activity. Ideally, experienced students will be able to critique Web site information routinely. However, to get to that point, a new teacher may need to begin by creating prompts or triggers to serve as review categories. This could be as detailed and complex as needed for beginning student researchers. A simple prompt worksheet might look like Figure 9.1.

Again, mentors should advise new teachers to adjust the level of guidance, triggers, and prompts to the experience of the students.

Box 9.1

---

1. Content

What is the purpose of this resource? Who is the target audience? What scientific claims are made? What information and content are available here?

2. Source Credibility

Who is publishing this page? Are there any potential biases or conflicts of interest?

How much support or evidence exists for the claims made within the resource? Is it referenced or academically cited to back up the claims or information beyond common knowledge?

3. Overall Organization

How well organized is the information? Is there a central page where everything is accessible? Are there links to other relevant Internet sites? How technical is the information?

4. Appearance

Is it a professionally designed resource? Do the graphics support the information and help communicate it? Does the resource "teach" the information?

Precautions and Possible Pitfalls

⚠ At its best, the Internet and its resources provide students with an easily accessible source of valid resources for a variety of curricular activities. However, it can also be a source of biased content and misinformation. Mentors should warn new teachers that Web site text can be copied and pasted into word processing programs. Some students will over-rely on the Internet and not use other more traditional resources. Teachers should be careful to make these points clear to students. Students should be encouraged to plan ahead to use other sources of information.

Source

Bos, N. (2000). High school students' critical evaluation of scientific resources on the World Wide Web. *Journal of Science Education and Technology, 9*(2), 161–173.

 STRATEGY 74: Encourage beginning teachers to develop student assessment alternatives that move beyond paper to electronic file cabinets and digital portfolios.

What the Research Says

 The Annenberg Institute for School Reform and the Coalition for Essential Schools, with the support of IBM, investigated the use of the digital portfolio at six schools. Digital Portfolio software was used to create a multimedia collection of students' work and connect the work to performance standards. The sites represented rural, suburban, and urban schools that were both technology rich and poor. Digital Portfolio software was customized for each school, and part of the effort included putting portfolio content online. In addition to the usual goals and objectives of the portfolio strategy, the aim of the digital portfolio was to expand the viewing audience to include college admissions and placement offices.

Word processing, scanning, and digitizing audio and video provided the means of entry into the multimedia portfolio. Researchers found the need for the targeted schools to support a schoolwide vision of how technology, and digital portfolios in particular, corresponds with the school's other systems. The main benefit of the digital portfolio in contrast to its paper counterpart seems to be its ability to become available to a wider audience. In addition, technology can add a few extra process steps that provide the students greater opportunity to reflect on and polish their presentations.

Application

 While a schoolwide digital portfolio requirement might not be realistic or feasible, a digital portfolio option may be just the right thing for specific classes, teachers, and students. Consider the following ideas:

- New teachers can keep samples of student work as examples of student mastery or the end product of the teachers' curricular activities.
- Allow motivated and interested students the option of a digital portfolio. A student artist or photographer could benefit by digitizing all his or her work, along with appropriate reflection and written content.
- Students interested in technology as a career could benefit by recording their mastery in the field as well as fulfilling a specific class portfolio requirement.
- A student could produce a digital job resume in portfolio form.
- Form a class portfolio and turn it into a class Web page that is available to a much wider audience.
- Include parents as collaborators and viewers in digital technology.

Digital media provide another vehicle for sharing student work. Because it is a relatively new idea, the limits of technology have not been reached. Creative students and teachers can experiment with new and innovative uses of the digital portfolio as it finds its niche within other instructional strategies.

Precautions and Possible Pitfalls

The research points to time as the major instructional concern. The technological learning curve has a huge time component, and the time needs to come from somewhere. New teachers cannot just add new requirements on top of their curricular goals and objectives. Mentors should try to help them make realistical time estimates to learn or teach any new technology and have them be prepared to let go of some other parts of their curriculum or instructional activities.

Source

Niguidula, D. (1997). Picturing performance with digital portfolios. *Educational Leadership, 55*(3), 26–29.

 STRATEGY 75: Introduce beginning teachers to reliable teacher support Web sites.

What the Research Says

Teachers have more information available to them on the Internet to assist them in lesson planning, subject area content, and problem solving than ever before. As access to this technology grows, teachers must decide how best to use it. For a teacher who is new to the profession, it is advantageous to use information about best practices that is already available and has been used successfully by other teachers. *How People Learn,* a recent report from the National Research Council (Bransford, Brown, & Cocking, 1999), applies principles from research on human learning to issues of education. It is not necessary for every lesson, strategy, and activity to be original. Teachers by their very nature are sharing individuals, and there are many Web sites geared specifically to assist new teachers.

Application

No doubt many beginning teachers feel overwhelmed by the scope of their chosen profession. Collaborating with a mentor or colleague can help ease some of the frustrations and problems new teachers may encounter. They may also gain insight and ideas for lessons and classroom management tips from a seasoned veteran. But what about after school hours or when a teacher is home alone at 10 p.m.? Where can a new teacher turn for help and advice from other teachers? The Internet has changed the way we communicate, socialize, shop, and stay informed. There are also some Web sites geared toward helping new teachers succeed. Sites such as Teachers Helping Teachers (www.pacificnet.net/~mandel) is by teachers and for teachers. Its goal is to provide to beginning teachers some basic tips that can be used immediately in the classroom. The site offers lesson plans and a list of educational Web sites organized by subject area and topic. The Beginning Teacher's Tool Box (www.inspiringteachers.com) is a site operated by veteran teachers of the Inspiring Teachers Publishing Group in Garland, Texas. This site offers everything from "Ask Our Mentor a Question" to Tips for New Teachers. Included in this site are words of inspiration, humor, and a list of the top 10 things to do before school starts.

Over 2,000 lesson plans organized by grade, subject, and key word can be accessed at the PBS Teacher Source (www.pbs.org/teachersource/search.htm). All content areas are represented and teachers can see how the lessons match many national, state, and district standards.

There are two Web sites that are a "must" for the new teacher. First is Kathy Schrock's Guide for Educators (discoveryschool.com/schrockguide), an extremely comprehensive site that hosts a wide range of topics that are organized in a user-friendly manner. The second is a site that every teacher, beginning or veteran, should know about. The U.S. Department of Education's Web site, The New Teacher's Guide to the U. S. Department of Education (ed.gov/pubs/TeachersGuide), provides a wealth of information free of charge.

Precautions and Possible Pitfalls

The use of the Internet in the past few years has changed the way teachers view the world. While there is a plethora of Internet Web sites catering to teachers, students, and education, it is important for the mentor to help the new teacher to navigate and process the huge amount of information available. Mentors may want to preselect favorite examples of Web sites that support beginning teacher development. Care should be taken to determine the validity of site information while allowing teachers a practical look at the information presented.

Sources

Bransford, J. D., Brown, A. L., & Cocking, R. R. (Eds.). (1999). *How people learn: Brain, mind, experience, and school.* Washington, DC: National Academy Press.

Eckman, A. (2001). Web wonders: Teaching the Internet generation. *Association for Supervision and Curriculum Development Bulletin, 58*(2), 96–97.

Kelly, L. (1999). Web wonders. *Association for Supervision and Curriculum Development Bulletin, 56*(8), 83–84.

10

Supporting New Teachers as They Develop Positive Relationships With Parents and Community

You cannot teach a man anything; you can only help him find it within himself.

Galileo

Unless one has taught . . . it is hard to imagine the extent of demands made on a teacher's attention.

Charles E. Silberman

Treat people as if they were what they ought to be and you help them to become what they are capable of being.

Goethe

STRATEGY 76: Help beginning teachers prepare for the specialized requirements of placement in an urban multicultural setting.

What the Research Says

This study (Barry & Lechner, 1995) examined a group of preservice teachers' awareness and attitudes about various aspects of multicultural teaching and learning. The group consisted of 73 students enrolled in undergraduate teaching methods classes at a large university in the southeastern United States. The majority of the subjects were white females. Surveys and questionnaires were primary sources of data.

Results indicated that these education majors were aware of many issues related to multicultural education and anticipated a diverse classroom experience in their future. Most were undecided and had little confidence (60.3%) as to just how well their teacher preparation had developed their abilities to teach children from cultural and religious backgrounds other than their own. This included communication with the students' families. However, 49% felt confident in their ability to locate and evaluate culturally diverse materials. The major recommendations and conclusions focused on education programs and coursework discussing potential changes and alterations to teacher training curricula and pedagogy.

Application

Often people look to colleges and universities for expert opinions on a wide range of topics. Academics make a living creating new knowledge and act as repositories of the most current thinking on many of today's major issues. However, new teachers should not necessarily find security in their ability to train for a multicultural experience. Research suggests that there is a wide range of competency within teacher education programs nationwide.

Most new teachers are culture bound and have little experience looking at life through the eyes of other ethnic and religious cultures and socioeconomic levels. The most common suggestions coming out of the research for teacher candidates or preservice teachers centered on individuals volunteering for service or finding a local, knowledgeable, nonjudgmental mentor in school districts a teacher thinks he or she might apply to. Both suggestions can be arranged in any number of ways, both formally and informally.

The teacher can ask school personnel in the district for suggestions on how best to become prepared. Another suggestion focused on selectively picking faculty in a teacher education program that offers the most realistic help in preparing a teacher for placement in ethnically sensitive settings.

A beginning teacher who plans to apply or suspects he or she will be applying to multicultural urban schools can take a proactive role in seeking out the right kind of help before becoming disillusioned because of a lack of preparation or naïveté.

Precautions and Possible Pitfalls

Mentors know that there are not too many pitfalls in becoming more proactive in these matters. It is no secret that ill-prepared teachers become very disillusioned about teaching and their career choice. Teaching is hard enough without underestimating the potential rigors a new teacher might face in unfamiliar settings.

Source

Barry, N. H., & Lechner, J. V. (1995). Preservice teachers' attitudes and awareness of multicultural teaching and learning. *Teaching and Teacher Education, 11*(2), 149–161.

STRATEGY 77: Encourage beginning teachers to make an extra effort to recruit minority and culturally diverse parents into the educational mix.

What the Research Says

America's schools face greater diversity today than at any time in our history. During the past three decades, schools have taken in great numbers of students from Laos, Cambodia, Vietnam, and the Philippines. With families from Mexico, Central America, and the Caribbean, along with immigrants from China and Korea, all coming to the United States seeking more favorable job options, politically stable environments, and educational opportunities for their children, America's schools have never been more diverse. In Los Angeles Unified School District (the second largest in the United States), students speak some 80 different languages.

Studies of Latino immigrant families repeatedly show that the parents are highly interested in their children's education (Goldenberg & Gallimore, 1995). These parents, although they may be unfamiliar and uncomfortable with the American educational system, display a strong desire to see their children succeed and want to contribute to this success. Research on parents of minority and low-income students suggests they would like to be much more involved than they currently are in supporting their children's schools (Metropolitan Life, 1987). Studies including African American parents report the same high interest but find that many of these parents lack the confidence that is necessary to support involvement (Chavkin & Williams, 1993).

Application

The face of an American teacher is typically female, Caucasian, and monolingual. This reality poses some interesting challenges for involving parents of minority and culturally diverse parents in the education of their students. The beginning teacher may feel somewhat apprehensive in recruiting parents of minority and culturally diverse students as resources in the classroom. This reluctance is based on a concern about language difficulties, possible cultural differences, or simply inexperience on the part of the new teacher. And yet, because of our changing population, the beginning teacher should expect a diverse population of students. The challenges now facing teachers in these diverse settings may occasion the need for social understanding that goes beyond the aspects of culture often approached in teacher education multicultural classes. Challenges include the proper handling of major holidays, religious customs, dress, and food. Even veteran teachers express a need for more intensive kinds of insight into the social ideals, values, and behavioral standards of each culture. They also require a more firm understanding of these standards and the cultural approaches to child rearing and schooling, first in the parent's own culture and then in the cultures these parents have passed down to their children.

Many new teachers focus on critical thinking and Socratic questioning techniques, which emphasize a student's active class participation (usually verbal). If students are from a cultural background that stresses quiet respect in school, they may need to be coaxed to become more active participants in their own learning. Teachers can speak with parents about why active participation is important to their child's education. Teachers can also provide alternative opportunities, such as allowing students to write journal entries or interact in small-group discussions.

Following are some suggestions new teachers can use to make their classrooms more culture friendly and to promote students' values of helping and sharing:

- Select two classroom monitors representing two different cultures and encourage them to work together.

- Allow students to help each other study vocabulary (students with greater English proficiency help those with a lesser ability).
- Allow students to work in small groups to preview their homework assignments, discussing possible strategies for problems and ensuring that all understand the assignment. This also helps students whose parents may not be able to read the assignment in English.
- Use a variety of reading techniques (pair reading, small group, lit circles, etc.).
- Provide opportunities for a variety of assessments (tests, oral reports, videos, posters, skits, etc.).
- Emphasize joint ownership of classroom materials.

Precautions and Possible Pitfalls

Parents of culturally diverse students can be an untapped resource in today's classrooms. Care should be taken to keep parents informed through communication (either written or oral) in the parent's native language if their English is not proficient. The beginning teacher must also be aware that even if he or she sends home information in the parents' native language, the parents may still not be able to read or write in that language. It is not uncommon to find parents who have had no formal education. The more information teachers can have about their students, their family, and their cultural identity, the better teachers can work with parents in supporting students' learning.

Sources

Goldenberg, C., & Gallimore, R. (1995). Immigrant Latino parents' values and beliefs about their children's education: Continuities and discontinuities across cultures and generations. In P. Pintrich & M. Maehr (Eds.), *Advances in achievement motivation* (Vol. 9, pp. 183–228). Greenwich, CT. JAI Press.

Metropolitan Life. (1987). Study of minority parent involvement in schools. Cited in Chavkin, N. F., & Williams, D. L. (1993). Minority parents and the elementary school. In N. F. Chavkin (Ed.), *Families and schools in a pluralistic society* (pp. 73–83). New York: State University of New York Press.

Trumbull, E., Greenfield, P. M., Rothstein-Fisch, C., & Quiroz, B. 2001. *Bridging cultures between home and school: A guide for teachers.* Mahwah, NJ: Lawrence Erlbaum.

 STRATEGY 78: Remind beginning teachers to expect a wide range of working conditions, as all schools and school districts are not created equal.

What the Research Says

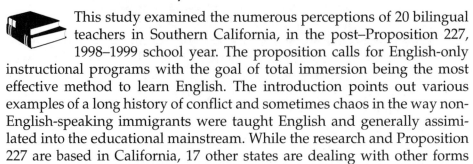 This study examined the numerous perceptions of 20 bilingual teachers in Southern California, in the post–Proposition 227, 1998–1999 school year. The proposition calls for English-only instructional programs with the goal of total immersion being the most effective method to learn English. The introduction points out various examples of a long history of conflict and sometimes chaos in the way non-English-speaking immigrants were taught English and generally assimilated into the educational mainstream. While the research and Proposition 227 are based in California, 17 other states are dealing with other forms of English-only legislation, laws, or guidelines. The researcher states that many bilingual teachers are seen as "marginal teachers" who must teach those "foreigners" who refuse to learn English. This then contributes to the bilingual teacher feeling isolated, alienated, and under intense scrutiny.

In-depth interviews and a questionnaire produced data to hopefully shed light on the following themes:

- The subject's rationale for the advantages and importance of bilingual education
- Whether their students had experienced any academic setbacks resulting from Proposition 227
- Parents' reaction to the initiative
- Parents' rights
- Any notable changes in attitudes of non-bilingual teachers and staff toward them and their students
- The extent to which they had followed guidelines or used loopholes to engage in resistance behavior

The stories told by teachers in the study were of beliefs, values, frustrations, challenges, and the ethical and curricular dilemmas they encountered in teaching language-minority students. Overall these teachers reported that Proposition 227 had created chaos, confusion, and academic setbacks for students and had intensified animosity between bilingual and non-bilingual advocates.

Respondents did show resilience and continued commitment to bilingual education and saw a role change to facilitators of reorganization. The teachers in this study also showed resistance and contestation behaviors to the mandates. They understood the hostile environment created by Proposition 227 and acted as insulators and protectors for their students.

Application

 Mentors know that in a typical staff dynamic, certain teachers emerge as leaders and zealous advocates for their programs and their students. This is accomplished usually by shear force of professional personality within a teaching staff. These leaders make it a point to line up administrators, both at their school and at the district level, with parents and community leaders behind them. The resulting formal and informal power base works to cement a program together and creates a resiliency that protects and maintains their program. This type of presence, within a staff, changes minds and goes a long way in placing their program in a positive light. Not every new teacher is capable of establishing this type of program aura, however.

New teachers need to realize that most good, effective programs are the result of individuals. These individuals didn't just fall into the program; *they are the program,* and if they leave, some or maybe all their power and the program may go too, or at least drastically change.

As a part of a potentially marginalized educational program, new teachers can make a difference. However, the playing field, as presented in the research, is not even for bilingual programs. Understanding the politics at the site, regionally, and at the state level is an important start. The origin of most problems is both inside and outside the classroom.

Mentors know that teachers' students, curriculum, and pedagogy do need to be their first priority, but the job requires teachers to do more. Teachers will need to advocate for the resources and an equal standing for their program within the power structure of the school institution. Unlike other content teachers, bilingual teachers will need to do more and often deal with more frustration and greater challenges.

Empowering limited or non-English speakers is a noble and necessary act. It is part of a long thread that connects the history of the United States. There is a rich history of language-minority students who have benefited and contributed socially, economically, educationally, and culturally. School has always been a source of socialization strategies for language-minority students. However, career bilingual teachers need to understand going in how public and professional sentiments shape and often send confusing and frustrating messages to those in the trenches.

Precautions and Possible Pitfalls

For a new bilingual teacher coming out of college or a university, school culture shock can set a lifelong view of school or teaching. It is important to realize that there are huge differences among schools and districts in the treatment of bilingual programs. If new teachers happen to land in a bad program or find themselves working with bitter or burned-out teachers, they must realize that there is a bigger world out there. New teachers should do their homework by gathering as much information as they can before applying for a job in a district.

Sources

Balderrama, M. V. (2001). The (mis)preparation of teachers in the Proposition 227 era: Humanizing teacher roles and their practice. *Urban Review, 33*(3), 255–267.

Valdez, E. O. (2001). Winning the battle, losing the war: Bilingual teachers and post-Proposition 227. *Urban Review, 33*(3), 237–253

STRATEGY 79: Remind beginning teachers to be prepared to help parents understand media coverage of educational issues.

What the Research Says

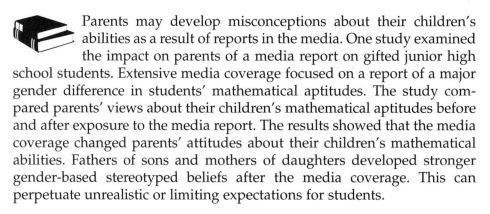

Parents may develop misconceptions about their children's abilities as a result of reports in the media. One study examined the impact on parents of a media report on gifted junior high school students. Extensive media coverage focused on a report of a major gender difference in students' mathematical aptitudes. The study compared parents' views about their children's mathematical aptitudes before and after exposure to the media report. The results showed that the media coverage changed parents' attitudes about their children's mathematical abilities. Fathers of sons and mothers of daughters developed stronger gender-based stereotyped beliefs after the media coverage. This can perpetuate unrealistic or limiting expectations for students.

Application

Many students find one discipline or another to be particularly frustrating. Many parents react by saying that they didn't do well in that subject themselves, so they tend to accept this from their children. Sometimes it appears to be a sort of badge of honor to admit weakness in science or mathematics (unlike almost any other subject). Beginning teachers can participate in periodic workshops for parents, illustrating what is being taught, how it is being presented, and what can be expected of students, both in performance and in results. This sort of workshop experience will also give teachers an opportunity to communicate with parents regularly and to inform them of their individual child's progress and ability to be successful in whatever discipline is being taught. Parents will then be more prepared to interpret reports from the media and other sources. These same parents would also be less likely to succumb to overgeneralizations and stereotypes that could undermine their child's performance.

Precautions and Possible Pitfalls

 Extreme patience must be used when working with parents. New teachers should recognize that many parents may have been away from a school setting and the concomitant behavior for many years. Beginning teachers should be cautious when reporting on a student's progress. Mentors should advise them to leave room for improvement and never close the door on an individual student, no matter how frustrating the child's progress may be. It is especially important to remember that some parents have a tendency to overreact to the teacher's comments, and that may have deleterious effects.

Source

Jacobs, J. E., & Eccles, J. S. (1985). Gender differences in ability: The impact of media reports on parents. *Educational Researcher, 14*(3), 20–25.

 STRATEGY 80: Tell beginning teachers what their teacher education program didn't tell them about parent-teacher conferences.

What the Research Says

 A questionnaire was developed to determine preservice program requirements relative to information and skills for parent-teacher conferences. Of the 136 teacher education institutions questioned, 124 institutions responded.

The percentages of those that frequently required preparation for parent-teacher conferencing are listed as follows:

- Elementary: 59%
- Early childhood education: 57%
- Special education: 44%
- K–12/all levels: 42%

Of the responding institutions, 19% provided and required a separate course for parent-teacher conferences. Seventy-five percent indicated that these skills are taught in a methods course context. Seventy percent included parent-teacher conferencing content and skills in field-based experiences.

Despite renewed emphasis on parental involvement, preservice programs did not consistently identify parent-teacher conferencing skills as a major objective. Field-based experiences address the topic but appear hindered by school policies in actual conferences.

Application

Many new teachers do not feel prepared for parent-teacher conferencing. Many veteran teachers avoid and are not comfortable in these situations. Experience is the best teacher. If a beginning teacher does not receive a background and a basic understanding of parent-teacher communication techniques, he or she may need to look for other sources of information on effective strategies. Learning on the job by acquiring information from colleagues can be helpful. Beginning teachers can also search academic literature, where there is an extensive knowledge base.

Parents come to the table with their own agenda, and the new teacher is usually there to react to their concerns. Occasionally, a teacher can react positively to their concerns about the student. Most of the time teachers are in a position that requires them to mitigate and litigate the student-teacher or student-curriculum-pedagogy relationship. Occasionally, the new teacher is called to defend his or her practices. Mentors may want to provide the following list of suggestions that can help:

• Collect phone numbers and addresses and identify early which parent the students would like the teacher to communicate with. This includes work phone numbers. Put the information on file cards. This lets students and parents know the teacher is willing to be proactive in communicating with home. If a student's last name is different from his or her parents, making sure the correct last name is used can be critically important in establishing rapport from the beginning of the conversation.

• Let parents know how they can best reach the teacher, through telephone calls, e-mail, or other strategies. Teachers can send the information home by mail or announce it during open house. The smart teacher will create a returnable parent acknowledgment of receiving the information and reward the student.

• If appropriate, the teacher can make his or her calls during school hours with the student present. After the teacher has spoken to the parents, parents often want to talk to their son or daughter. This works well with behavior problems. Students usually want to avoid these situations. Once a new teacher does this, the rest of his or her class will quickly get the message that parental relationships are important to the classroom teacher.

• Teachers should acknowledge potential trouble early and become proactive. The teacher can avoid getting calls by making calls home first. Often the call parents make won't be to the teacher; it will be to someone in the administration. A call at the first sign of trouble can often clear up misunderstandings early.

- It is important to realize that the classroom experience the student is taking home is filtered through the mind of that student. Teachers need to itemize and break down the potential issues ahead of time and prepare a response. Acknowledge the concerns the parents bring and prepare to redefine them from your perspective. It is helpful to remember that the teacher and the parents are on the same side, collaborators in the students' education.

- As a "new teacher on the block," try to talk to counselors, administrators, or other teachers familiar with the student before making calls or conferencing with parents. Sometimes even veteran teachers need help in dealing with certain parents. Teachers shouldn't put themselves in a position to be ambushed. If a teacher is really worried, it is perfectly okay to have a counselor or administrator familiar with the parents present and to let the parents know that he or she will be there.

- Sometimes it might be better for a teacher to let others familiar with the parents and student make the call. The teacher can then set up a conference if it is still necessary. A teacher shouldn't see this as a sign of weakness. It can be the best strategy. A vote of confidence directed toward the teacher by a trusted counselor or administrator can get around the school's community quickly and begin to build the new teacher's reputation as a caring and effective teacher and communicator. This can be a really necessary strategy for non-English-speaking parents.

- Once in a parent-teacher conference, the teacher should start the conference by listening carefully to what the parents have to say. Having itemized grades, lessons, handouts, student work, and so on will help. The teacher can then break down parent concerns and carefully address each one individually. Being organized and prepared ahead of time with potential solutions to the problems a teacher expects to hear can reap rewards in increased communication and rapport with parents.

- Letting supervisors know ahead of time about problems that could spill over into their laps allows teachers and supervisors to work on strategies together. Giving the supervisor copies of relevant materials (classroom policies, copies of tests, etc.) in advance so they are brought up to speed can help make the new teacher's job easier.

Precautions and Possible Pitfalls

Many times parent conferences are positive experiences. However, they can also turn sour. Occasionally parents simply will not be there for the teacher or their son or daughter. They may not have control over their relationship with their child themselves. Mentors know that phone calls home and parent conferences may be a lost cause in some cases. Counselors can often alert the teacher to situations where conferencing won't help. A new teacher could end up listening to the parent's problems and never really resolve the issues with the student. In these cases, the teacher will need to follow through on the paperwork the school or district requires such as sending home notifications. However, sometimes new teachers may need to accept the fact that they should work with their mentor to come up with strategies that won't include the parents.

Sources

Henderson, M. V., Hunt, S. N., & Day, R. (1993). Parent-teacher conferencing skills and pre-service programs. *Education, 114*(1), 71.

Rabbitt, C. (1984). The parent/teacher conference: Trauma or teamwork. *Phi Delta Kappan, 59,* 471–472.

> *STRATEGY 81: Help beginning teachers examine the complex issues surrounding parent involvement in schools.*

What the Research Says

The author begins with the premise that research has shown consistently that with an increase in parental involvement, there is an increase in student achievement. From there he moves into data gathering at four high schools, one public school in Indiana, an urban public school in Southern California, a parochial school in Central California, and a public school in Central California. These schools represented a diverse community and student mix typical of high schools these days. His goal was to characterize the perceptions of teachers, parents, and administration relating to school-parent interactions at the secondary level. For the purpose of this study, 50 teachers (25 males and 25 females), 25 parents (20 females and 5 males), and 8 administrators (3 male and 5 female) were interviewed to investigate the phenomenon of parental involvement. Barriers to parental involvement that came from teachers included stereotypes that teachers had about lower socioeconomic parents and single-parent families.

Concerning at-risk families, many teachers were apprehensive and desired parental involvement to be limited to school functions and at-home activities. Many teachers felt that parents were not professionally able to contribute on school (curriculum)–related committees.

The issue of communication between home and school was a major theme for parents. Most teachers and parents interviewed expressed strain in parent-teacher relationships due to lack of communication. Teachers and parents also felt fear and insecurity toward each other. Some parents stayed clear of teacher communication and focused on their student's counselor. Other parents felt arguing with a teacher or administrator might bring on subtle repercussions targeting their student.

Research conclusions (as cited in the paper):

- The study found that the majority of participants commented that better communication needed to be developed between teacher and parents.
- Both teachers and parents felt the other group was responsible for initiating dialog.
- More senior teachers made negative comments about parents, while younger teachers mentioned parents in a positive light.
- More opportunities for parents to be involved would bring more positive interactions.
- Teachers and administrators paid lip service to the idea of parental involvement in curriculum development.
- Teachers, administrators, and parents verified that the majority of contacts home were to report negative situations rather than supportive reports.
- Most teachers reported avoiding calls home due to the number of students they have.
- Mailing information home presented problems in areas of limited English proficiency or illiteracy.
- The parents in this study felt they were caught in a situation in which they were portrayed as "nosey or a problem" if they became involved or "not caring" if they didn't.

No suggestions to remedy the situation were made. It was only made clear what the problems were. Although the literature search found a positive correlation between parental involvement and student achievement, the results of the study point to parent-school communication as a less than maximized factor or strategy in education.

Application

It is clear from the study that parental involvement is an ill-defined concept, especially at the secondary level. Chances are that the new teachers were not trained in education classes to understand the complexities of parental communication. It is also reflected in the research that experienced teachers have a more negative view of parental interaction. The dilemma for many teachers is how to implement strategies to improve communication with families or involve families yet feel the extra workload is not being placed on their shoulders alone. Teachers do not like to use the telephone to communicate with parents because parents are often hard to reach and teachers don't like to use their evening hours talking about school issues with parents.

Mentors should remind new teachers that they are not just doing a job; beyond that, they are also advocates for the children. Also, some of these parents are continually "in the process of losing their dreams of what their children will be and facing the reality of who their children are becoming." This is not always the case, but negative contacts tear away at the dreams they have had for their child.

Acknowledging and understanding the feelings of loss and grief that accompany this process can "change the way we deal with parents." This is especially true when calling students' homes to discuss disciplinary or academic issues.

Beyond the ultimate goal of supporting students, schools benefit when teachers strive to understand how parents feel and to validate those emotions. "A parent who feels that he or she can walk into a school and be heard by the administration and by the teachers will leave that school and say, "They listened to me."

When parents don't feel that their voices are heard or doubt the teacher's perspective, they will exercise some power where they can. Teachers, counselors, and administrators have to work hard to develop constructive, productive relationships with parents. New teachers need to develop strategies to identify and avoid the language and behaviors that alienate parents.

Here are some suggestions for positive contacts:

- Create opportunities for parents and allow parents to learn about opportunities for parental involvement at school and at the district level and get involved if at all possible.
- E-mail communication works well because, unlike the telephone, no one needs to be in one spot to receive it. Use e-mail to:
  Create parental lists for mass mailings of course-related information.
  Send homework home for the week.
  Dialog with specific parents as needed.
- Web sites have come into vogue lately, but many are not current because it requires time to keep them up. New teachers can train a student to maintain their page or ask a computer literate parent to volunteer.
- Occasional home mailings/newsletters of relevant material can help keep parents up to date and in the classroom loop.
- In addition to back-to-school nights, sports night, and other parent-school interactions, one high school created an "Academy Award" night. Each teacher and department was able to nominate a set number of students for excellence within the various disciplines.

There were some monetary awards also. Seniors were presented awards in a separate ceremony. Ultimately over 200 students out of 1,500 were recognized for positive accomplishments.

- During back-to-school night ask for potential mentors, speakers, and donations where parents can become more involved in your discipline or department.
- The new school year comes with hope for success. It's a new beginning. Everyone cooperates. Disappointment comes with the first telephone call bearing bad news or the first report card. The parents' initial reaction is to question the news, and fear may enter their minds. Without some understanding, denial, blame, and evasion set in. With a positive intervention from a teacher, hope can be restored and the parents become willing to listen and accept help from the school and the teacher. The result is a positive relationship and mutual appreciation.
- School-parent interaction is a team game. A teacher new to an assignment can benefit from talking to others who might know their student before contacting the parents. A new teacher can name-drop a trusted counselor or administrator. The parent will know that the teacher has networked and is not working with his or her student in isolation.

Mentors can be especially helpful in encouraging new teachers to apply whichever strategies appeal to them.

Precautions and Possible Pitfalls

If mentors keep parental interaction at a distance, it may be not in the new teacher's best interest to transmit these negative feelings about parental communication. The study cited did show that veteran teachers were less likely to present a positive attitude regarding parental interaction.

Like homework, parental communication is not done on a level playing field. Once students leave the classroom the opportunity to succeed is not equal and they will be going home to parents who may or may not be involved in their work as students. Parents are not created equal. It is important that students are not discriminated against overtly or subtly based on the involvement or lack of involvement of their parents.

Source

Ramirez, A. Y. (2001). "Parent involvement is like apple pie": A look at parental involvement in two states. *The High School Journal*, Oct/Nov, pp. 1–9.

Index

**CORWIN
PRESS**

The Corwin Press logo—a raven striding across an open book—represents the union of courage and learning. Corwin Press is committed to improving education for all learners by publishing books and other professional development resources for those serving the field of K–12 education. By providing practical, hands-on materials, Corwin Press continues to carry out the promise of its motto: **"Helping Educators Do Their Work Better."**